Luther Theological Seminary

ST. PAUL, MINNESOTA

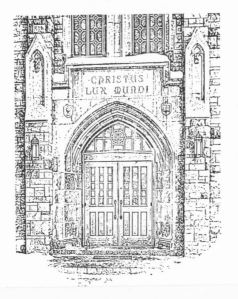

Death's Single Privacy

Death's Single Privacy

Grieving and Personal Growth

JOYCE PHIPPS

A CONTINUUM BOOK

The Seabury Press · New York

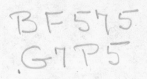

The Seabury Press
815 Second Avenue
New York, N.Y. 10017

Copyright © 1974 by Joyce Phipps
Designed by Paula Wiener
Printed in the United States of America

Library of Congress Cataloging in Publication Data

Phipps, Joyce.
   Death's single privacy.

   (A Continuum book)
   1. Bereavement—Personal narratives. I. Title.
[DNLM: 1. Death—Personal narratives. 2. Grief—
Personal narratives.   BF575.G7 P573d 1974]
BF575.G7P48   155.9′37 [B]   73-17881
ISBN 0-8164-9203-4

To those who have
shared their lives with me

Contents

Death's Single Privacy

✦ Introduction

The Circumstances of Death

The day my husband died had not followed its usual pattern. Because I had not been able to get a babysitter, I did not go to a monthly meeting in Hartford. Instead I found myself ironing and glued to a reenactment of "Surrender at Appomattox." When the phone rang I thought, now why couldn't that have happened during a commercial. The voice at the other end of the line said, "This is Lisa. Could you come up and get Mr. Phipps? He isn't feeling well." I thought, boy, when Bob admits he's not feeling well, something must really be wrong. On the way out I passed a friend dropping off some materials for a League of Women Voters meeting the next morning, commented that I had to go and pick up Bob since he wasn't feeling well, and started out on the less than half-mile drive to the college. There are advantages to living so close, I mused, somewhat resenting the fact that I always had to pick Bob up after those Monday evening seminars because Bob did not like driving at night.

Driving around to the far side of the campus to bring the car as close as possible to the library entrance, I passed a fire emergency truck going in the opposite direction. "Huh," muttering to myself, "wonder where he's going."

When I pulled the car around and hastily got out, I saw that same emergency truck in front of the library. A sharp pain shot through my body, my thighs throbbed, and all I could think was "heart attack!"

Running over to the building, I saw one of the librarians with an expression that said: "My God! It's your husband." A fellow student, seeing me at the front door, said she would look after the children so I could feel free to go to the hospital. The elevator was on hold for the fourth floor. Bounding up the stairs as if climbing one flight, I turned into the hallway to see stunned expressions on the faces of Bob's colleagues. The students were at the end of the hallway, around another corner. They were all standing, staring into the room with horrified expressions. I swallowed hard, walked into the room, and saw Bob on the floor. The first words I heard came from a nurse: "No pulse! No pulse for ten minutes!" One of the emergency truck men nudged her, she looked at me, and then the attendant said, "Don't worry, everything's going to be just fine."

I sat down in one of the chairs. Just fine? I looked round at all the people. Lisa, the student who had called me, offered to go home and watch the sleeping children. "Go ahead. You'll meet Jean there, but if the boys wake, they won't know her." I looked back at the floor. The impressions were so clear, so vivid. The body on the floor, bloated and stomach distended. The face, expressionless, pale, already turning blue. I stood watching for several minutes. The ambulance was on its way. I searched out a custodian who opened an office so I could call a minister.

"Nancy Jo? This is Joyce," I began, clearing my throat, preparing to say what I already knew was true. "Listen, Bob's had a heart attack, and I think he's dead. Could you and John meet me at the hospital? . . . Yale-New Haven," I added as an afterthought. She said they would. Coming out I was told that I could not ride in the ambulance "because of the equipment" and decided to drive myself. A student nervously volunteered to ride with me. "Are you sure you want to drive?" he timidly asked. "What do you want me to do," I snapped back, sorry even as I was talking for the tone of my voice, "twiddle my thumbs?"

The ambulance passed us halfway there but Nancy Jo and her husband, John, had arrived before the ambulance. Nancy Jo, one of the associate ministers of my church, was standing at the entrance with John. Her face belied her words of hope, that "they" were working on him, that there had been some response. I looked around the lobby, partly in curiosity, partly to feel some kinship with someone else. But faces turned away from me, one by one, as I looked into the eyes of the other persons in the waiting room. After filling out the necessary forms we went into a small room with a bench around two sides of the room and an examining table in the middle. A woman in a white dress came in, fidgeting with a small manila envelope. She kept her eyes to the floor, not saying a word. When asked what was going on, she replied, "The doctor will be here soon. They're working on him." Somehow I felt the sudden urge to scream at her that you don't "work on" a person, but I remained silent. I knew that he was dead. I was searching for some substantiation of what I knew to be true. Then the doctor came in.

The doctor was a hospital resident, taller than Bob, with strawberry blond hair, in his mid-thirties. His name tag was on his pocket. He looked like he wanted to avoid the situation. Incredible, that the impressions were so very, very clear. He looked around the room, saw me, and began, "Mrs. Phipps? We did all we could. Your husband —he p-passed a-away—just a few moments ago." He paused. I could almost hear him saying to himself, "I did it. I told her. What will she do?"

"You mean, he's *dead*." That word was so necessary to use. God, I thought, is this a time for avoiding the use of real words? "Yes," came his response, in a tone half-apologetic, half-fearful, that somehow he had failed. "He is d-d-dead." He seemed surprised at himself when he said that word. "We did all that we could." The nurse jutted out her hand like a mechanical doll, handing me the manila envelope. "You'll have to sign for these," she explained. I looked at the list of contents: coins, Timex watch, one yellow metal wedding band, $1.12 in loose change. My eyes fixed on the "one yellow metal wedding band." Is this what's left? I signed, half smiling. I turned to the doctor, looked at him, put my hand on his shoulder, thinking, Jesus, it's a good thing *I* can handle this. He sure can't! "I know you did what you could. Thank you." Then looking at Nancy Jo, I said, "We'd better go. It's going to be a long evening."

I thought about that doctor and nurse. As a society we avoid death whenever possible. Had Bob's death been his first death experience, or had he felt failure professionally, or did seeing a man just thirty-six years old threaten his own sense of mortality? This had not been a freak accident but had been a death from "natural causes," which is far more threatening.

Nancy Jo nervously got into my car—I insisted on driving. Somehow I seemed to be "in control." John dropped off the student back at the college. We came into the house. Looking directly at Lisa, I simply said, "He's dead." She fell into my arms, sobbing, and we held on to each other very tightly. Jean, about fifteen years my senior, came forward with an "I'm so sorry," told me she would call me the next day. Then they both left.

"Well, I'd better call Marian." Dialing to suburban Washington, I wondered what my sister would say. "Marian? This is Joyce. Listen. Bob had a heart attack tonight,

and he died." "Joyce?" came the response, "are you kidding me?" "No, I'm not kidding. Call Mommy and Daddy.
[My deaf parents have a teletype telephone to be able to
call Marian whenever they need her.] Tell them what
happened. The memorial service will be on—" and interrupting myself I asked Nancy Jo, and then resumed,
"—Thursday. Call me back." "Sure will," came her char-
acteristic response. The phone started ringing within a few
minutes. Within another twenty minutes the house was
full of people.

Looking back, it seems very strange what I could and
could not do. I could comfort the students who burst into
the living room in tears; I could serve up enough Scotch to
sink the navy to Bob's departmental colleagues; I could
embrace them all, agree how terrible it all was, even crack
some jokes (Bob had been no sourpuss!). But I could not
call his sister in Ohio. I felt as if I hardly knew her, having
met her on only two occasions (our wedding and their father's heart attack, death, and funeral), and I feared her
response and that somehow I would not be able to
"handle" her. Interesting how we think of "handling"
people—like the doctor "working on" Bob. Nancy Jo
called her for me. She collapsed at the news. She then
called back in a few minutes. Then I could talk to her and
tell her what happened, tell her about the details, etc. She
promised to call me back in the morning.

We had hardly gotten through the family phone calls
when the doorbell rang. The departmental chairman and
a delegation from the history department had arrived. I
sat them down, all squeezed together on a couch not comfortable for three grown men, and broke open the Scotch.
The spread of the news was incredibly fast. Students who
had gone to a student party told others who were there
who then told others. They all ended up in my living
room that night. A student of Bob's who was also a faculty

wife called another faculty wife with whom I was good friends. She called others, and they all came. The children slept through a total of sixty-odd persons that evening. The senior minister of my church arrived and we set up times, schedules, and talked about arrangements. I called the funeral director, agreed to meet with him early the next morning.

Immediately I was thrust into a decision-making capacity. There were the decisions about details: times, places, who goes where. These detailed decisions were but reflections of the decisions on larger issues: How would we treat death? What would I tell the boys in the morning? How were they to be involved? How would we deal with Bob's death in the general community and make this death an experience to be seen in a religious framework? As the evening developed, and as we all talked, some of the decisions began to crystallize in my mind.

Most of the people left by midnight. Nancy Jo offered to stay with me, but I felt it was important to confront the aloneness immediately, to face the empty room myself. The other associate minister, who had been at the meeting I missed in Hartford, had arrived by eleven or so, and we talked after everyone else had left of how I felt about what had happened in light of my emotional and psychological makeup and mindset. That year of marriage had been a hard one in which I had begun to deal with issues raised by the women's movement. Bob had been a gallant chauvinist in many ways, and in many other ways a chauvinist not so gallant. "Why now?" I cried out. "Why when things were going again?" "You do have that, the knowledge that you were talking, communicating, really working through your life together," he answered. "Yes, I've got that, knowing that through all the hassles, the marriage was worth the hassle," I agreed, looked at him, sobbed out of anger, desperation, fear, and love. I thanked him for the use of his shoulder, noted that it was after one o'clock in the morning, and said good-night. I looked at the living room. There was an immediate sense of spatial increase. I turned out the lights, walked toward the bedroom, paused at the door of the children's room, thought, so that's how I'm going to tell them, undressed, and got into the empty bed.

1

Telling the Children

How do you tell two young children that their father is dead? What on earth was I going to say to a five-and-a-half-year-old and his almost three-year-old brother? How was I going to be honest in my answers to their questions and keep some sense of security for them? I decided to tell them the simple direct truth as I understood it in simple direct language. I had already made the decision to do it alone, within the confines of our nuclear family, as the only adult present, so that any ambivalences they would sense from others later could be referred back to the original explanations and their parameters. Several decisions stood firm: to be open-ended, to explain the separation of the live person from the dead body, and no "viewing" of the body in a casket. The reasons for these decisions came partly out of my own uncertainty about what is called "immortality" and "the hope of the life to come," as it is so often expressed in the language of the church; partly, from my disgust with what seemed to be body worship in many traditionally done funerals, where the spirit of the person seemed lost; and partly, out of the conviction that the body I had seen on the classroom floor had only been the dwelling place of that open, warm, and magnanimous spirit known as Bob Phipps.

It was imperative for the children to see Bob's death as a final separation, that Daddy was not simply off somewhere else, that Daddy had not just "gone away," as one young child once said to me of his father, that Daddy was really dead. I was determined to use that word "dead" and then remembered that even the doctor could not bring himself to use that word. The words we do use, "deceased" and "passed away," are really quite nonpersonal. "Dead" and "death" are quite personal. Societally, we seem to prefer the nonpersonal. Perhaps it seems less threatening to us.

The morning after Bob died, I woke up earlier than the boys. Perhaps I had not even slept that night. I got out of bed, went into their room, pulled the younger one onto the older boy's bed, swallowed hard, held onto them, and said, "I have something very sad to tell you. Your Daddy had a heart attack last night at school, and he died." I stopped. I was suddenly aware that I was crying. Keith, the older boy, stared in disbelief. He had seen animals die. He seemed to have some idea of what I was saying. He blurted out, "Who's going to take care of us when you're not here? Who's going to be our babysitter?" His facial expression indicated his fear of the unknown. Daddy had been the babysitter normally. Daddy had been there when needed. "Keith," I responded, "whenever I have to go out to a meeting, I'll get you a sitter you know and like, like Susan or Laura. There will always be someone to take care of you and Craig." Craig just started muttering, "My Daddy die . . . my Daddy die?" I grabbed them both, held them tightly for what seemed like a very long time and yet like a split second. Keith pulled back, looked at me very intently, realized this was no joke, and started the questioning: What's a heart attack? What causes them? Did it hurt? Did Daddy die without pain? How did I know for sure he was dead? Did I *see* him die?

His questions reflected his anxieties: how could I, the

mother, be sure that someone was not just putting me on unless I *saw* him die? That one point became extremely important in the establishment of the credibility of the story to him. He needed assurance that his Dad had not just been snatched off and that I had not then been fooled into believing that he had died. His quest for details seemed endless: Exactly how? Who was there? Exactly how long? Who babysat while I went to the hospital? (Security again!) How did I know that it did not hurt? Why could the doctors not help? For almost an hour I answered the same questions over and over again, trying to keep my words consistent. Keith finally broke loose from me and ran into "our" bedroom to check me out. Craig just sat on my lap, muttering again and again, "Daddy die . . . Daddy die . . ."

I had often heard that young children at different ages dealt with the news of death differently. In that two and three-quarter years between the two boys there was the beginning of the understanding of the word "dead." Occasionally, Keith had found dead birds and mice, done in by our cat, and the pain in those deaths had been obvious to him. At these instances I had explained what happened to the bodies of these dead animals—that in decaying they became part of the earth and helped to make things grow again. Birds, mice, and a pet gerbil—in terms of their bodies—became like the fish heads buried under newly set out tomato plants. To Craig the word "die" was a new addition to his rapidly expanding vocabulary.

We adults often try to "shield" children from death. Theoretically, we are protecting them from grief. My observation has been that we are really protecting ourselves from their probing and often brutal questions. Because we ourselves are uneasy about our own deaths and about the deaths of others we have set up polite ways of referring to the "departed" to the point of almost denying the reality of death and often, as the result, confusing the grieving process. We as adults have created a conspiracy of silence which denies to children the right to work through *their* grief. So often adults will comment that a child is obviously "over it," because "he's happy" or "he's playing" or "he never talks about it." Little wonder, since the surviving parent and family give out the message by their pained looks that the children should not ask questions. A child sensitizes himself not to say anything, not to ask, not to emote, not to cry, or to cry along certain proscribed lines.

When a child asks, "What happens to a person when he dies?" and the adult questioned is uncomfortable about either the question or the answer he gives, the child is usually sensitive enough to pick that up. To be able to say honestly to a child, "I don't know" beyond the description of the actual occurrences, or to be able to discuss the varieties of religious beliefs people hold about death, preparing the child, in a sense, for the varieties of beliefs he will be confronted with, is critical in establishing the child's trust of the adult at this time. When a child senses that an adult is lying—"covering," in our adult terms—he understandably will be quite concerned, adding even more of a burden to the insecurity the adult is already dealing with.

And the actions of adults should reflect the beliefs they pass on to their children. An elementary school girl once observed that if her mother had really been "taken by God" to a place as fine as heaven, then she could not understand why her father's grief had been so intense. And it is for precisely this reason that adults try to "protect" children from their outward appearances of grief. As a result, however, what the child senses from all this is that death is a topic not to be discussed. The situation normally ends up with repressed adult grief, confusion on the part of the children involved, and a total breakdown in communication at a time when some form of communication is so vital.

Of course, not all communication is verbal. So often we

feel we cannot communicate except verbally, but just being together, sharing some experiences, with an attitude of openness and mutual trust, constitutes communication of a sort. The survivors just holding on to each other constitutes a form of communication. One father communicated his grief and was able to share it with his sons by playing baseball with a determination and an intensity as to seem almost pathological to the casual onlooker. However, he and his two boys were communicating their grief which they felt they could not speak of because they did not have the words to articulate it.

My own response to Bob's death was to tell my children that Bob was dead and that burial of the body was required for health reasons. I also mentioned that the body itself was not the person we had known and that some people had bodies cremated rather than buried. I did not use the word disposal in reference to the body, however, because young children also hold on to something tangible. This explanation had been corroborated by our previous experience with dead animals; the boys had been absolutely prohibited from touching dead animals with bare hands. We had always picked up the animals with paper and buried them in a back section of the garden.

I also explained that this burial required a great deal of work, both legal and financial, that just as it was important in the life of a community when a baby was born to make this fact known to the community, it was also important to do the same thing when a person dies. We celebrate the birth of a baby as a community experience, as a religious experience. We would also offer a thanksgiving for the life that had been, in the form of a memorial service, to create a community experience, to understand the life in terms of fundamental experiences. There is a difference between faith and a set of beliefs. Faith is the understanding that casts life in terms of certain perspectives. We as a community and as individuals normally use a religious framework for that understanding. We all share faith, I told the children, but the beliefs that structure the faith, and that reflect the varieties of perspectives, differ from person to person, each set of beliefs valid for the people involved, as long as those beliefs are really reflective of the faith and are meaningful for the person holding those particular sets of beliefs.

I made the distinction between the body to be buried and the living person they had known as Daddy. That open-endedness seemed very necessary. I felt that I should not limit their understanding of what had happened by my own uncertainties about what death means, nor should I shape their thought in terms of particular images and symbols which might prove to be limiting to their future religious development. I knew that to discuss death in my adult language with children as young as these would be utterly meaningless. They needed concreteness. They needed language which would be suitable to their thought and abstraction capabilities. Very often adults talk of heaven as an honest attempt to bring their adult understanding of the world down to a child's level. And then the child takes it literally. One five-year-old had been told that her mother had gone to heaven, and that she had become an angel, and that it was true in our terms that the young girl would never see her mother again. The child then proceeded to try to write letters to heaven and to her mother though she accepted, seemingly, the idea that she would never see her mother again. A burial of the letters was required, the child was then talked to more honestly, and a long process of working out the confusion arising from the misunderstanding began.

I told the boys that many people would be very sad for many different reasons. Some people would miss Daddy because he would not be around to add his two-cents'-worth to a conversation, a meeting, a dispute. Some would miss his sense of humor, the way in which he had been able to differ with people without making such differences into personality battles. Some people would cry. Some would not. The boys should feel free to cry but *they did not have to cry if they did not want to*. I told them they could talk to anyone they wanted to about the death, ask any questions, but to remember that many people were afraid of death, were afraid of dying, because life is so beautiful, and because in life people have some chance of controlling the situations in which they find themselves. Loss of that control and the fear of the unknown, I told them, lay behind the avoidance of death.

When Nancy Jo arrived about eight o'clock that morning, Keith looked her straight in the eye and said, "Did you know my Dad died last night?" Nancy bent down to his eye level and gently said, "Yes, I know. We're all very sad." She then went on to tell Keith how she had felt about Bob, who he had been in her life. I was pleased that their first outside experience had been supportive. She would talk to them on their level, and her openness toward their questions was picked up right away.

The flurry of activity was about to start. I asked Keith whether he would prefer to go to school or to go to a friend's house. He chose the friend. And at this friend's home all day he kept up his process of verification. Each new person entering he would query: Did you know my Dad died last night? Let's make sure they're not putting something over on me. Sadness. They look like they're going to cry. Separation. Finality.

Craig also stayed with a friend that morning. The friend's mother reported much the same response, just not so well articulated. He took to crushing dandelions, repeating the word "dead" after each act of violence.

I felt it was important that the boys' memory of their father be the living vibrant person, so I decided against their "viewing"—and that word choice is interesting in itself—the body in a casket. My decision not to view the body myself was partly based on the feeling that if in years hence the boys wanted to know if I had seen Daddy's body when they had not, I would be able to answer that I had not, that all things had been equal.

I had also decided against a "wake"—a term applied to receiving friends in a funeral home. I wanted my children totally immersed in the grief of the community. I was concerned about doing this in a place where I would have to worry if they were into things, in a place where they would be uncomfortable, in a place where the attitudes and real feelings of people are so often constricted. The funeral director was able to tell anyone who called to call at the house which would be open to all—friends, faculty, students, political acquaintances, in short, anyone wanting some sense of shared grief.

The response of the boys to the opening of the house was incredible. Keith would question each newly arrived mourner, carefully study his or her face, and more and more the reality began to sink in for him. This was indeed a significant event. "Wow, Mom, did Daddy really have this many friends?" he asked at one point. Later, while with two dozen people in the living room we were all trying to get some dinner, he looked up at the door with glee: "Here's someone else who loved our Dad!" He wanted to greet each new arrival himself, hug them, love them, hear them stumble into words of condolence. He was able to realize a sense of the community, which grieved when one important to it had died. The community comforts itself—and the community in the midst of its sorrow can still find joy and laughter within it, especially in remembering amusing incidents that members have shared. Still later that evening, from his bed, he would yell into the living room, "Who's there now?"

On Wednesday he wanted to go to school. He asked if I had talked to his teacher. I answered that I had. He wanted to know what her response had been. Did the principal know? Do all the neighbors know? He checked it all out before heading off. He openly discussed it with all the neighborhood children, and the children responded quite openly. I walked with him halfway to school that morning, concerned about his responses. When we got to the crossing guard who told Keith that she was sorry that his Daddy had died, he turned around with, "Gee, I'm glad a lot of people miss my Dad." He could hardly wait for the arrival of the grandparents and his Aunt Marian.

The children were a concern of mine in planning the memorial service. As part of this total immersion I felt they should be present at the service. That meant I had to make it short, plan familiar music, and keep the Bible readings simple. Bob's favorite hymn—"A Mighty Fortress Is Our God"—would be sung; they knew it well. The service would close with what had become our household's secular hymn, "We Shall Overcome." The Bible readings included the Good Samaritan which they knew from a small Archon book. I asked people the boys knew to deliver the three thanksgivings (for the teacher, the churchman, and the man committed to political and social change), and that they be short.

The body was to be interred in a city some two-and-a-half-hours' drive from New Haven. I was concerned about the strain of the drive and the interment. I felt that the situation in Brockton would not be entirely within my control, and that stability would be the key to security during this week. So I decided against their going, though I did ask if they cared to go. However, the way in which I asked the question loaded the dice, so to speak, and I knew their answers would be no.

Concerned with how the children would query my parents and sister and her husband, I decided that I would lay out how I had handled the situation up to the point of their arrival, making it clear that I hoped they would go along in certain respects, mainly in terms of openness.

The boys met Bob's sister for the very first time the morning of the memorial service. They did not seem to relate to her in any real person-to-person way, understandable under the circumstances.

The morning of the service, we all arrived early at the church. Some friends ran the boys all over the New Haven Green both to tire them out so that they would sit for forty to forty-five minutes, and to exhaust some of the accumulated nervous energy. Because I was standing out in front of the building, not wanting to sit down until absolutely necessary, I ended up welcoming those coming. We finally came in together and sat down front. Keith looked around the sanctuary. It was packed, he observed. "Hey, look at her. She's crying." I whispered an answer, "Yes, she's very sad." Both children smiled and waved at people, who for the most part waved back. Ensconced between Grandpa and myself, Keith began to squirm a bit. But he listened intently to the Good Samaritan story, responding with a raised hand and a very loud "I know!" to the question Jesus asked of the young lawyer: Who was the neighbor? He searched around with his eyes. I kept feeding Craig more paper to draw on. Keith looked at me when Bob's best friend in the history department delivered the thanksgiving for the teacher. "He's talking about my Dad," Keith said quickly and nervously. "I want to go home. I'm getting sad." I bent over explaining in a whisper why it was necessary that he stay: Just look at those people. See them? If you get up and run out now, they will all break down and cry. They *need you* to help them remember how thankful we are for your Dad. Then Keith noticed Grandpa, staring ahead at the interpreter into sign language, brushing away a tear, "Hey, Mom, look!" he practically shouted; then he whispered, "Grandpa's crying!" Grandpas cry only when something is very sad indeed.

As the three of us walked out during the last verse of

"We Shall Overcome" Keith broke down on the church steps. I sat down on the steps, held on to him very tightly. In a moment it was all over. He started running around, seeing all our friends, talking to them, laughing, teasing other children. Craig was looking for the papers he had been drawing on. I watched the boys and wondered when the real outbursts would come.

Since those days I have heard a number of adults who had lost their parents when they were young talk about their experiences as they remembered them. One young woman told me of the sensation of having had her father simply disappear. She remembered a pale and wan mother who never discussed her father's death or her father after he died. The little girl had not been involved but "protected," and another relative had explained the whole thing to her as "your father's gone to heaven." Only in this woman's adulthood has she been able even to raise questions about her father. Her memories are somewhat bitter, and she still cannot bring herself to talk to her mother about her father's death.

More recently, a woman whose husband had been killed in a boating accident related that in the four years since the event, she and her son, who was in the boat when her husband had drowned, had never discussed the event. She had told her son to tell his friends that he did not care to discuss it if they asked him what had happened. When she asked him exactly what happened, he turned round on her, stating that he "did not care to discuss it."

Very often adults have ideas about how children will respond to a given event such as a death. Usually, they assume children will respond like adults. "What's the matter? Why don't you cry?" screamed one anguished parent, not understanding his child's stony silence. Openness seems to be that quality which allows both child and surviving spouse to express their grief in their own individual ways. Constant discussion is not necessary, but the option for discussion should be there. Different children respond in different ways, according to age, environment, cultural milieu, and clues received from the adults around them. There seem to be ages for silence, as well as ages for talk.

Keith and Craig talked constantly about "it." Keith's kindergarten teacher told me Friday morning, the day after the memorial service, "We didn't tell the other children what happened because we didn't want to upset them." Wow, I thought, is this for real? What on earth did she and the principal think those children were talking about? There were some parents who reacted in much the same way. But Keith took it out from under them during his "sharing time" with the simple statement the next Monday morning, "My Dad died last week." The children in the classroom discussed death and dying for almost an hour. The teacher, who reported how "astonished" she had been, eventually had to cut the discussion.

This constant discussion continued throughout the first few weeks and beyond. It seemed almost inevitable—though as a person with some historical training, I usually avoid that word—that much of the talk would concentrate on theological ideas, that is, explanations within the context of religious experiences. I was particularly concerned about how the boys would "handle" death, how they would assimilate it and integrate it into their life experience and use that integration as a base for future orientation.

A cemetery lay between our house and the college. Keith had noticed burials from time to time, asking me what that all meant. He had noticed how alone and isolated the bereaved had looked. Among my bad habits is that of picking up hitchhikers. One morning we picked up a young woman, and Keith asked her, "Did you know my Dad?" She looked at me, then at the children, who resemble their father a great deal, and stammered, "You're Mrs. Ph-Phipps." Then she started to cry. My immediate thought was, of all the eleven thousand students at the college, we have to get one of Bob's students. Craig started asking, "Why she crying, Mommy?" Keith simply leaned forward, put his hand on her shoulder, and said, "That's okay. We all loved my Dad." He then proceeded to relate how all the various communities involved had functioned and how they had all intersected. She was fascinated. I myself was stunned. Her parting comment was, "I wish my religious experience had been that open and nonthreatening."

I thought about her words. Yes, rather than hassling through sets of beliefs and having to relate them in a context which wiped away half his world, he had seen people talk of how his father had touched their lives, how his life would have a deep impact on their lives though they would miss him very much. I realized that the reason that Keith could be accepting of all the shades of religious beliefs was that none of them affected the way in which he viewed his father.

Within that first week, Keith came in and told me that the boy next door had told him that his mother had had a mass said for our Daddy so that his soul would not burn in purgatory. "What's purgatory?" he quickly asked. I gasped, then took hold of myself and started with something to the effect of: "Remember how we talked about that picture you saw [some medieval piece] with all the people and the devils?" "Yes," came his reply, "but you said people used to believe that stuff a long time ago." I paused, catching my breath. "Ah, yes, I did. But just because some people believed some things a long time ago doesn't mean that some people still don't continue to believe them." I went on to explain that no one really *knows* whether or not such things happen to people after they die. Just as I do not know whether or not that quality which divides the living person from the dead body is more than "life" as we experience it, so others do not know either. People hold different beliefs, though, positive and negative, about that quality called life. Some people believe that all life stops at death and that there is nothing beyond what we experience on this earth; this constituted a belief, not knowledge. Some people believe that the quality of life is something like a spirit—not a ghost, but like our thoughts and feelings, not something you can touch but something you can feel and know is really there. Some people have even more detailed sets of beliefs, such as the existence of places to which this quality of life actually goes after death: heaven—a word we use when we want to say being with God; purgatory—a place where souls (the name we often ascribe to the quality of life) go to be cleansed of sin (that which makes us do bad things or think bad thoughts); and hell—a place utterly without hope. At that point, Keith broke in with, "Oh, Mommy, you said a bad word." I then explained that the reason "hell" was a bad word was that it meant a place so utterly terrible and hopeless; to tell someone to "go to hell" means wishing the worst on that person.

Keith was intrigued with the possibilities of such beliefs. "But," he asked, "how do they know?" "The fact is, they don't, just as I don't. But people have such beliefs," I answered, "because either they were brought up with those beliefs, or they came to believe them because that's how the world makes sense to them." These beliefs are meaningful and valid for the people who believe them; they give credence and validity to those people's lives. What is sad is clutching on to beliefs no longer meaningful within a life context. People do this, I explained, because they fear the consequences, that is, they fear their lives will totally be without meaning. I put this fear in terms of the brokenness of the world, that people are not complete in and of themselves but only within the context of something beyond themselves, within community, only within sharing and giving to others. When people attempt to be complete in and of themselves, they sense that they are not and then use religious beliefs to give them a sense of completeness. That is why they are so threatened when their beliefs are challenged. Such challenges pierce their view of themselves and their place in life.

"Do *you* believe in all that stuff?" Keith asked, and rather uncomfortably I responded, "All which stuff?" It is always easier to discuss religious feelings in terms of what other people believe rather than in terms of how you yourself feel. I realized that it was taking time for me to internalize and integrate my intellectualized gropings into my system. "Heaven!" he shouted. I told him that I did not know what that quality of life was which had been in his father, but that I felt that that quality had been shared by the gerbil which died, indeed by every living creature. I went on to explain that what counted for me was not a set of beliefs about purgatory, heaven, or hell, but how people lived, how they touched each other and cared for each other and expressed that care; that the way in which people lived could be considered to be reflective of their faith. I then asked him if he really felt good about himself when cut off from his friends, his group, those whom he loved. When he answered no, I continued, saying that the very need to love and to be loved was indicative of our incompleteness, and to be complete we needed to be interdependent with each other. Then I said that I did not live in the hope of a life to come because that seemed to be wishing my life away, and what mattered to me was that we all live and try to live as well as Daddy had. No, I did not believe in "heaven," because I had no reason to. But I did not "not believe" as well. No one had ever come back from the dead to tell me whether there was a heaven or not. I told him I felt people had "invented" heaven (not as a lie, but as an explanation) in order to come to terms with what it was that happened when a person died and the life seemed to disappear and all that was left was a body.

This kind of discussion continued for days. Then, about a week and a half later, Keith came in, announcing defiantly, "I believe in heaven!" One of his friends had told him that heaven was "really real." I was amused because the parents of the friend in question were avowed atheists. It suddenly occurred to me that Keith needed something more than community experience. He was really afraid of totally losing his father. Though our shared experiences had been necessary, the conceptualization of them did seem amorphous and abstract to him. "Fine," I said, "believe in heaven if you want to. That's your right."

From the very beginning I was concerned with what the boys, being so young, would remember of their father. A friend, who was six years old when his father died, told me of his experience. His mother had created a "memory book" in which the children could write their memories of their father or have their mother write them as they talked. I saw the importance for us of having such a memory book, since in this way our feelings, griefs, remembrances, and shared experiences would get talked through, integrated, and internalized. The remembering and talking, the recreating of the experience, and the expression of feelings about the experience did indeed serve as a catharsis. We also found ourselves sorting photographs into an album before the end of the first week.

Adults outside our family responded to their perceptions of grief in my children in many ways. The Friday of the week that Bob died Craig was playing with a friend. A visitor commented, "See, he's already over it. Look at him play." It seems that external behavior is often totally unrelated to what goes on inside a person. Craig had not "gotten over it" but, in truth, had not yet begun to grieve. All that week he would repeat constantly, "My Daddy die," as if to say, tell me, now, what does that really mean? why isn't my Daddy here? Another visitor commented that Craig's "constant preoccupation" with the fact that his father had died was "morbid."

Keith asked why his father had died. I explained the causes of death in natural terms. Heart attacks were linked to blood circulation, cholesterol, overweight, and smoking. I further explained that most people never really think they are going to die so they never really believe what the doctors tell them, such as that smoking is bad for your heart, etc. When my sister arrived from Washington, she lit up a cigarette, and Keith was horrified, "Aunt Marian, don't you know that's what killed my Dad?" Poor Marian! She dropped the cigarette, was obviously shaken, picked it up, and put it out. When she started up another one about fifteen minutes later, she commented, "Well, I don't think that smoking is bad for everyone. There are other factors, you know." Keith impatiently and pointedly commented that his Dad had always made the same claim.

For Keith and Craig, the main impressions of the significance of the death of their father were formed within the first week. They had absorbed the tenor of the community, the language everyone around them had used, and their responses as well. Just before my sister left with my parents and her husband to go back to Washington, she commented that the community had really been great. Keith looked up at her and said, "It's this way, you gotta love to be loved, and you gotta be loved to be able to love."

2

The Socialization of Death

The third phone call the night Bob died had been to the funeral director. It is strange how different people approach this aspect of death. I remember the first time I saw a body "laid out" in a casket as a child of six or seven. Visually, the impression was one of a dimly lit room with a bright white light either in front of or behind the casket. The body seemed to be of the same bright whitish tone. Everyone walked around in a hush, and there seemed to be an aura of mystery. Above all the one impression that remained was the sense of distance that people had from each other; they did not seem to behave in their normal manner with each other. There seemed to be more distance among the living than between them and the dead.

Adult experiences confirmed this impression, one which crossed all denominational lines. When my grandfather died I was expected to make all the standard and traditional responses, but I refused. I wanted to scream out in frustration at what seemed to be happening. But as I watched, I began to realize that funerals are for the living, not for the dead. A few years later when my grandmother died, I happened to come to the funeral home late. My parents were with a few friends. "Aren't you going to view the body?" they asked. "View"—another distancing word. I practically had to be forced into the room, muttering

under my breath that I did not want a remembrance of
her corpse obscuring the memory of what she had been to
me alive. That same year a young friend, my own age,
died from multiple sclerosis within a year of her college
graduation. I was somewhat curious about a Jewish funeral home: what would be different? what would be the
same? Bob and I were both relieved to find a closed casket.
But as intimate as we had both been with this young
woman and her newly widowed husband, the whole atmosphere of the funeral home created a barrier between us,
put masks on us all. When we arrived at the home, after
the burial, the masks were removed, and we were all able
to see each other as responsive individuals, something we
had been unable to do in the funeral home.

Bob's father had died the spring that the Nancy Mitford
book, *The American Way of Death*, was published, and,
having read it, we both approached the funeral director
with what we considered to be a very healthy skepticism.
But though the masks assumed in this case differed greatly
from those above, the masks were there just the same. Old
New England Protestant and Irish Catholic traditions con-
verged in terms of the grief displayed toward the body in
the casket; however, there was the same distance between
people, even brother and sister, in the funeral parlor. Two
years later a great-uncle of mine died, and, there again, in
even another kind of cultural setting, the mourners were
cut off, one from another, in the funeral parlor. As these
impressions rushed over me, I began to plan what I hoped
would be a different kind of experience for my children,
Bob's family and friends, my family and friends, and the
community surrounding us.

Somehow I was surprised—though it seems strange in
retrospect—that the funeral director could see us as early
as 8:30 A.M. The boys wanted to know what a funeral director did. We lived near a cemetery, and the boys had
previously expressed curiosity when they had seen a cor-

tege arrive or a grave-opening machine at work. I had explained in terms of others, and now explained again, in terms of Bob's body, that bodies, when the life had gone out of them—that the bodies of dead persons—had to be buried or cremated as a protection against disease. A mortician prepared the body for burial or cremation. The buried body would become part of the earth again. The mortician protected the mourners and the society at large against the possibility of infection. "Oh, you mean like a doctor," commented Keith. "Yes," I agreed, "somewhat like a doctor." I was careful not to detail the exact methods of embalming though I did make it quite clear that it entailed some procedures similar to surgery. As I talked to the boys I remembered that Bob's father had not permitted an autopsy on his own wife because he "didn't want her cut into." At that time I had asked Bob, "What on earth did he think a mortician did?" I felt that the physical aspects of handling the body of a dead person should be separated from the emotional attachment to the person once alive.

On the way downtown I told Nancy Jo my feelings about funeral parlors. She commented that most people had ambivalent feelings about them; they made the mental and emotional connection between funeral parlors and their "atmosphere of death" rather than perceiving that it was their own sense of isolation and detachment from others that they abhorred. I looked at the big old house and asked her why funeral parlors always seemed to be in old Victorian houses, unless it was to convey a kind of spooky atmosphere. I stepped back from myself, thinking wryly, at least I still have a sense of irony. Then I really stepped back from myself and wondered how hackneyed my expressions would be by the end of the week.

An older man answered the door and pointed out the direction in which we were to go. (It took some time before I realized that the woman I presumed to be the secretary was the funeral director's wife.) On the way upstairs, I looked at the bland wallpaper. "Where did they dig that up?" I whispered to Nancy Jo. "It's neutral," she said. Suddenly it struck me. The funeral parlor is supposed to be the neutral place; it is the institution American society has created to put distance between people so that they won't directly confront death and the grief in themselves and others. As I thought back on my previous experiences, I remembered being cautioned as a small child not to ask any questions about the man who had died because it might cause his widow to cry. In some sense, what I was cautioned against was feeling with another human being, against sharing the emotional involvement of grief. I remembered another time, how scandalized people had been when I threw myself into a young widower's arms in an attempt to break through the neutrality of the funeral home atmosphere and behavior.

Somehow I had expected shock or surprise when I explained why there would be no wake: the children needed to see the grief of a community in surroundings secure and familiar to them. I would not have the distance, the neutrality between people. This would be the time for growing closer, for real sharing. But the director, instead of looking like or acting like something out of Evelyn Waugh, not only seemed receptive to my ideas but welcomed them. I wanted to avoid any sense of intimacy with him, however. Ours was to be a business relationship. I realized that even with my minister by my side, my head quite level, I was not very emotionally stable.

I tried to concentrate on the details. And there were plenty of details to absorb me. It seemed that it took more paperwork to bury a man than to marry him and bear his children. Though there was this paper, that paper, the other paper, there did not seem to be the sense of rush that I had sometimes lived my life in. I seemed to have a sense of calm detachment. I wondered if this sense of detachment was a form of protection against the emotional intensity of grief.

Though obviously it was a mortician's business to be aware of the kinds of death benefits paid by various levels of government, I was impressed with his knowledge. First he asked all the expected questions: veteran status, Social Security status, whether or not disabilities were service-connected. He advised me to file for Social Security survivor's benefits as soon as possible because of the three-month (or more) lag in obtaining these benefits. He advised obtaining extra copies of death certificates because of the number of times I would need to have such certificates.

I told him that the burial would be in Bob's home town, Brockton, Massachusetts, but that I was concerned because Bob's sister or my parents, both of whom were traditional in their views on death, might want to "view" the body. He agreed to keep the body at the funeral home until the morning of the memorial service. Anyone who called the funeral home would be given the home phone number and told to call there. We made the necessary arrangements and I signed all the papers applying for all the possible death benefits.

We went into the coffin room, and I chose the simplest, second least expensive cloth-covered box, wondering how when one's husband were dead one could really care whether the lining is peach apricot or apricot peach. How could anyone spend a lot of money for a coffin, I wondered. Then I remembered our experience when Bob's father had died, and how Bob had spent an extra $900 on a coffin because the "wood was so beautiful," how someone had remarked that "Billy had never had a piece of furniture so fine." I could really feel with the need then to be concerned with the way in which someone would "look" in orchid or peach. Now I just wanted to get away from all those coffins. After all, I thought, I wouldn't be seeing Bob in a coffin; I would not even see the body. On top of all this I felt the societal pressure to "do justice" and "show respect" for Bob. I was relieved when the funeral home door closed behind us and we were in the early spring air again. "Let's get out of here," I remember myself saying. I talked about the funeral director, how expensive this was all going to be, how I would manage financially, and how the week had not yet really begun.

The obituary was in the Tuesday afternoon paper. When the phone calls came in, I vacillated between answering the phone myself and having someone else "run interference," as a friend termed it. The doorbell seemed to be ringing constantly. The boys were very impressed by the number of people who were coming by and calling, all openly displaying their grief. One friend came over with a bottle of Harvey's Bristol Cream and a dozen absolutely perfect white roses. ("Here," she had said, handing me the sherry, "everyone's entitled to a good drink now and then.") Dinner, if the hectic sitting down and getting up every minute or so to go to the door could be called that, came very late. Students, faculty, political and personal friends all reached out to each other as real human beings sharing grief. There was no distance between us. We all grieved together.

As the situation settled down by eleven that night with only two dozen or so squeezed into the living room, someone raised the question of the format of the memorial service. Nancy Jo showed me a "thanksgiving" for a minister who had died the previous month. I took the format, a Bible, and the phone directory, retreated to the study, and started to work. I listened to the conversation downstairs as I typed out the service and the short biography to be included. I began to see the significance this death could have in our community, or rather, the series of communities somewhat apart but coexisting side by side, and the ways in which levels and layers could be brought together to meet and interact.

Bob had been basically involved in three kinds of work in New Haven: college, church, and politics. Discussions with persons to be in the service, to be ushers, began. I felt it extremely important that each separate group he had worked with see the breadth of the man who had died, that his time, interest, and concern cut through community lines.

A death can serve many purposes. In our fragmented society it often serves as one of the few times a family gathers together. Ironically, sometimes this very gathering divides a family, because of the stress created by the death. We seem to be a society which presumes certain modes of behavior, and often the presumptions are not reflective of the internal and emotional situation at hand. For example, we seem to believe that we are supposed to be "closer" to members of our real family, whom we often do not see except at weddings and funerals, than to intimate friends with whom we have grown and developed. The lack of closeness to any family member only compounds the stress of dealing with death and grief. So we find ourselves thrown into the pretension of behaving with our family as we would behave with our closest friends. I had observed the divisiveness engendered in families facing death, and I wanted to have Bob's death weave people together, not pull them apart.

Funerals and memorial services can only be for the living, not for the dead. Still, people seem to be cowed into acting in a certain way because the "loved one" would presumably have wanted it so. Sometimes that kind of excuse is used to justify certain courses of action. I found myself using it. When asked, especially by those persons who were ambivalent about something I had decided, I would answer, "because Bob would have wanted it that way." This kind of accommodation seemed easier than debating with people over my personal reasons for doing one thing rather than another. Unfortunately what often happens is that others will also impose that kind of argument on the newly widowed person to serve their own desires. And that, too, is perfectly normal. As C. S. Lewis once observed, in grief we think first of ourselves, then of the dead, then of others.

I saw the service as the expression of what Bob was to the community, and what the community, in all its facets, would want. Because it was a Protestant service, a religious experience in which Bob's sister, a converted Catholic, might not be comfortable, a priest was asked to sit with her. Because my parents are deaf and I wanted them to get the full impact of the service, there was someone to help them so they would know what was read, sung, and said. Because most of our friends had young children, there was child-care so they would feel free to come at a time when babysitters are hard to come by (10:00 A.M. on a school morning). Because many of our friends came to the service from many different backgrounds, there was a variety of music. However, all the music, the "eulogies," the scripture, all of these things had intensely personal meaning to me as well. Even in its social aspects, I felt that it was of the utmost importance to make the situation as confronting as possible, to work myself through it, to force upon me the reality of death.

It is a cliché but it is nevertheless profoundly true that people need to feel needed. This holds for those peripheral to the event as well as those central to it, though, in a sense, no one is peripheral to death. Essential to the social experience is the realization that every single person is important. Each student, each faculty member, each note, each phone call, each face at the memorial service—each is a reassurance that the loss is real to the world outside yourself.

After the memorial service, the burial, the return trip, and the dinner, after the sitting down and the drinking up what's left of the coffee—after all this comes Monday morning. One wakes up and realizes there is so much to do: call Social Security, write letters, pay bills, call lawyers, accountants, file papers, check bankbooks and checking statements. I called Social Security to find out about filing for "survivor's benefits," as they are called. The lady answering the phone asked what she could do for me. I answered, "I am a recent widow," then choked. The word "widow" stuck in my throat. "Oh, I'm sorry," she answered, then continued, "When did your husband decease?" "When did he do what?" I sputtered back. She answered, "But we never say 'die.' It's so upsetting. That sounds so final, you see." In her well-intentioned way, she was denying death's reality. I wondered what she thought death was—some kind of trip you take? I swallowed hard, gave the information requested, made an appointment to come in and sign the papers, and hung up the phone in dismay.

Next came the insurance man. The secretary would send the forms. Then the attorney and the accountant. Everyone has all the answers from his own perspective. In terms of what I ought to do about my insurance I received three different answers. My head spun. Where does one get neutral opinions? I made those kinds of decisions on the grounds of majority rule: when two or more of the legal and financial experts would agree, I generally followed their advice. The open-ended decisions were normally the most frustrating.

One concern was money—immediately available money. Could I use the money in the accounts and not be concerned about violating any laws? Luckily, yes, since the accounts were in our names together. I had only to produce a death certificate to get some savings certificates that only Bob had signed for. Having received the insurance money from the state of Connecticut before the end of the first week, I was anxious to deposit the check immediately. When I looked at the bankbook, it looked like so very much money, but almost immediately it began to go —the funeral director's bill, some outstanding bills we had owed. I was concerned about whether I would be able to hold on to enough to get me through my last year of library school.

The best financial—and emotional, as a by-product—advice I received came from the accountant who had prepared our income tax returns. It was very simple, yet very sensible: stay fluid. Keeping the financial options open meant several things: not cashing in one life insurance policy to pay up the house mortgage immediately and therefore leaving a sum in case I would happen to need it; not tying up other insurance monies in savings certificates but allowing maximum flexibility in case I needed it. This financial flexibility contributed enormously to my emotional flexibility. Though it meant I had to use Social Security for my house payments there was the certainty that *if* I needed a large sum of money at any time, it would be mine.

Everyone had advice, of course. It seemed that all my male friends had become instant legal wizards, not to mention financial wizards. In talking to other widowed women I found this to be generally the case. The assumption was that, "naturally," the woman knows nothing about finances, and is incapable of learning. In our family, I had always balanced the checkbook. In that I was fortunate. I discovered through talking to other widows that many women do not even know how to write a check, or where their important papers are filed, and what bank has the security box, or where the key to it is. Beyond the simple acts and events of financial management, there is also the emotional insecurity that accompanies such management after the death of the husband—or wife. Women seem to be put upon not to spend any of the insurance money, to "save it for the children." Men, on the other hand, seem to be put upon to keep earning money. Men are also the victims of sex stereotyping in that they are not normally given legal and financial advice, because "they know it all, anyway." These expectations often weigh very heavily on widowers concerned about making ends meet (and sometimes the strain to get child-care and the expense involved can take away much of the widower's earning power).

In Connecticut there is a process called probating a will. In any state, the will—if there is any—must be executed. This process takes time. Six months to a year is the standard amount of time for such execution in Connecticut. During this time the widowed person consults with the attorney, and often there are no prior agreements made between the attorney and the widowed about the nature of the fees charged. I trusted my attorney. Many young—and older—widowed persons find they cannot trust their attorney because they do not feel comfortable with him. It may be due to a patronizing attitude, or that hauteur that is often found in persons rendering "professional services." Worse than actually being fleeced or bled is the *feeling* of being fleeced or bled.

It seemed like I spent the first month endlessly tying up loose ends—a paper signed here, another signed there, a phone call to A, then to B, then to A again. All the paperwork and financial and legal matters had the emotional effect of reinforcing the *idea* of my new status. The first time I had to say or write "recently widowed," I balked. By the middle of May, some three weeks later, it came more naturally. Many of the firms with which we had accounts were notified. I felt the need to establish my own accounts, somehow as a symbol that I was alive, that I was a person apart from my dead husband. By the end of May I was aware that I was developing a much wider, deeper, stronger sense of socialization which would involve my ongoing relationship with the community and my image of myself.

3

The Really Real

The perspectives of the surviving spouse and the surviving children seem to be very different so that often the parent does not make the mental connection between his own outward behavior and his internal emotions and the same dissociation in the child's comportment. The parent very often takes the approach of the outside world when it comes to being sensitive to his own child's grief. Quite often parents will talk about their children "getting over it" when they would take umbrage at such a statement made about themselves.

Only a few days after the memorial service a visitor, looking at Craig, then two and a half years old, playing with his favorite friend, commented, "Look, he's gotten over it already." "Gotten over it?" I queried. "Why he hasn't even begun to deal with it yet." It suddenly occurred to me if his favorite friend had been over and he had not played with him but had sat and moped, then there would be such a gross dysfunction evident that it would call for outside consultation.

There were, of course, ways in which the boys' behavior was not normal—their preoccupation with death, what it meant, whether they themselves would die, whether I would die, etc. For weeks there seemed to be a running contest between two life options for them in connection with me: would it be better to live with Aunt Marian, or would they really want me to stay alive? True, they would get to see Grandma and Grandpa more often if they lived with Aunt Marian. And Aunt Marian was nice, but so was Mommy. Understandably, it was difficult for me to be entirely detached from this discussion and to view it in terms of their understanding their own security!

What was Bob's death going to mean to them? How would that event, taken in the context of the response of the community, affect their thinking, their emotional development, their lives? No death occurs in a vacuum. Keith's responses were those of a five-and-a-half-year-old witnessing various events in a particular kind of community. Craig responded with the perspective of a two-and-a-half-year-old witnessing certain events. The perceptions of the boys differed from the very first day and changed at different paces. Their understandings developed differently; and their perspectives would naturally differ from those of other children within the same age group, even within the same religious denomination, since no two environments are precisely the same—not to mention the obvious fact that no two children are the same.

I expected that I would have to handle Bob's death differently with each of the boys. Just how differently I did not realize until a succession of individual occurrences seemed to form into patterns. Many times it seemed as though the moment I had discerned the patterns, the patterns changed. As the days became weeks and the weeks became months, however, certain dominant patterns did become clear. Craig spent the first few months trying to determine what this new word "dead" really meant. His method was simply to announce to people, "My Daddy died," and then to observe their responses in order to try to decide what his response should be. Keith, on the other hand, having already had the word "dead" in his vocabulary, seemed to be attempting to determine how this new situation changed his living patterns, his relationships with other people, and the community. Layered on top of these attempts to construe their own situations was simply grief at missing their father. Their own perceptions seemed to be the warp and the social context the woof of their fabric of experience; without either there would be no resolution of their confusion, and each helped to determine the effect of the other.

Children very often imitate their parents in working through their grief. At the time it seemed as though Keith never stopped talking about Bob, the death, the memorial service, how people responded. As I look back, I realize that he was trying to cope with these events in the way he saw me coping: by talking, by using each event as it occurred to force confrontation with what the death meant. Sometimes he shrank back, as I did; however, he seemed also, as I did, to put himself in situations which would demand an articulation on his part about this thing that had happened in his life. In the same way, Craig's announcement to people was his way of talking, his way of verbally checking out what this unknown reality meant. As I have met more and more people who have had to share their grief with young children and as I have heard them tell how their children have "gotten over it," I have come to the realization that the children very often were simply using the same defenses the parents had used. Talking is but one form of defense, one way of working out the sheer physical tension that arises from the death of a husband or wife, a father or a mother. Crying is another way of releasing that tension. In most cases, passivity and "bucking up" are not; such responses create dams between parents and their children. It takes a great deal of effort to constantly be breaking down those dams so that the streams which flow from the floodgates can give some indication of the quality of water which is behind them. Not only must that effort be constant but it is also very exhausting.

I had occasion recently to discuss a child's grief with his parent. "David and the rest of the children have gotten over it," this widower said, though he himself was still living as if in a state of shock months after his wife had been killed in an automobile accident. I can remember his face, utterly pained, and I pitied the children who probably feared discussing so painful a subject. He seemed to be oblivious to what I was trying to suggest, so I stood him before a mirror as I talked about his dead wife; the pain in his eyes was incredible. I said to him, "Look at yourself; and you want to know why your children don't talk to you. They won't even begin to because they see how it hurts you so."

I suggested he create situations in which there simply had to be some discussion—going through boxes of clothing in the change of seasons, for example. There are certain situations in which children seem to be reluctant to discuss the death with the parent. Part of this reluctance arises from the discomfort of age differences, especially for children around the age of puberty. Part of it comes from the strain of societal expectations imposed on the children. A parent sensitive to the differing responses of different ages can create situations in which children can discuss the events with those they feel most comfortable with. For boys an older friend, such as an uncle or a friend of the parents, and for girls, a young woman somewhere between the girl's age and the mother's age, do very well as confidants.

Keith talked because he knew he could. He heard me talk to the neighborhood children when they asked questions. He saw the openness with which I approached the subject, the way in which I accepted varieties of religious and nonreligious beliefs about what had happened. However, he also used the death as an instrument of rejecting authority, as do most children. His methods, of course, were peculiar to our own family situation. About three weeks after Bob died, when Keith came in and announced defiantly, "I believe in heaven," I assured him that that was perfectly all right, that his beliefs were entirely up to him. He immediately looked deflated, and I wondered if his assertion had been deliberately goading. I tried to separate the authority rejection of me from the attempt to keep Bob alive. Now as I look back I see they were interwoven and that even Keith could not have distinguished the various strains within his response.

I was preoccupied with maintaining the delicate balance between forcing the remembrance of their dead father on the children and encouraging them to be open. Sometimes I totally botched the situation by unwittingly using them to work out my own grief. Sometimes I reacted to outside pressures and overburdened them. One example of this was placing Bob's picture in the boys' room. As I look back, I wonder why I put that photograph, carefully chosen as it was, a picture of Bob in his office at school taken for the college paper, on the wall facing their beds. The photo did at times prove comforting, but eventually I could see his image increasing their nightly discomfort. As I discussed the bedtime tossing and turning with friends, one suggested that the photo had outlived its usefulness. I did not just take it down, leaving a hole in the wall, just as Bob's death had left a hole in their lives: I "redecorated" the room, shifting everything around, and when I was finished, the photo was gone, and their sleep seemed to be more peaceful. We had gone through weeks of nightly weeping, "feeling sad about my Dad" from Keith, before I had become sensitive to the problem.

The nightmares had started before the photo went up, however. One night I had heard Keith screaming shrilly, and I ran into his room. "Keith, Keith," I whispered softly, "what's wrong?" I could see the terror in his eyes, even in the dark. "I dreamed my Dad died," he said in a voice asking me to reassure him that his Dad was not dead, that everything was "all right." I choked. I shook him awake, brought him into my room, and said to him, "Keith, your father is dead. We all loved him very much, but he is dead." Keith looked around. There was no Bob in my bed. I asked him if he wanted to stay with me a while and he said he did. I felt sick and empty inside and held on to Keith tightly.

That first dream was the beginning of a series. It seemed that the whole world around him was dying—his friends, one by one, died in his dreams; his brother met death by a variety of means—and each time I would reassure him that this friend or that friend was in reality alive and that his brother was sleeping soundly on the bottom bunk. One night there was a scream more penetrating than any other. Keith was thrashing about, asleep, screaming something incomprehensible. I finally was able to shake him awake. "Keith, Keith, what's wrong?" He only shook his head and grabbed on to me very tightly, muttering something about my being there. The next morning he was either unwilling or unable to recount his nightmare as he had the others.

After Keith's nightmares stopped for a while, we went through a period of intense interest in our family life through photographs. I took all of the loose photos, separated them, arranged them chronologically, and we sat down together every night and pasted them in the album. People with no direct contact with death seem to be really uncomfortable with the idea of talking about the dead person. One hot afternoon I bumped into an old League of Women Voters acquaintance, and as we were talking, she asked what we were doing to "forget" and remarked how successful I appeared to be in my attempts. I was a bit startled, and commented that the boys had sent me to the stationery shop to pick up photo tab corners for assembling the album. "It's a bit early, isn't it, to do that?" I mumbled something about the boys wanting to do this and went out wondering what was meant by that statement. One thought that occurred was the avoidance of grief—the idea that if you wait long enough before dredging up the memories, the memories would be less painful.

I was very concerned that when Keith realized that Bob was really dead he should nevertheless still be able to view our family as a family, not a partial family or a "broken" one. As he would talk about Bob's death and the memorial service, I would say, "But what counts is the love we have for ourselves and others, and it's love that makes a family." The sense of security, of love, of family, seemed vitally important in keeping Keith as secure as possible while he went through his very painful realizations.

At times I would overhear Keith and Craig talking about what had happened. Keith would talk about Bob, what he had been in his life, and about how important that life had been, about how he missed his Daddy, about how we would do everything in threes, and so forth. Craig could not respond except by repeating "My Daddy died, my Daddy died." My pediatrician, an insightful man, who had called the day after Bob had died, had commented at the time that it would take a while for Craig to realize the full impact of Bob's death. I had not then realized what that meant.

One morning four months after the death we were getting ready to go to New Hampshire for a church camp, and Craig went one step too far by unpacking the suitcase for the third time, so I spanked him quite hard on his bare skin—a punishment reserved for very severe infractions of house rules. Craig collapsed on the floor, screaming, "I want my Daddy! I want my Daddy!" I stood open-mouthed. He clambered into my arms, crying, then sobbed with his whole body shaking. Keith heard all this commotion and ran inside, saw Craig, heard his cries for Daddy, and with extraordinary tenderness said, "Craig, our Daddy's dead." Craig stopped, looked up at him with a questioning look in his eyes, and Keith responded with, "It's true, it's really real." The boys just held on to each other.

Craig then started to go through some of the same external signs of grieving as had Keith—nightmares of losing his friends, his brother, and me; restless sleeping; sleepwalking; talking about memories. I suspected his memories of Bob were beginning to get hazy. He would always talk about what daddies did, how other children had daddies who did certain things with their children, but not of his own memories. He began to discuss death with his friends as Keith had discussed death with his friends.

I wondered what would happen when school started in September, how Keith would adjust without a father. Some of the older boys in the neighborhood had teased Keith about his father's death, and this was a cause of real worry. I tried to suggest that the boys who talked in this fashion were ignorant. However, that kind of consolation does not lessen the pain. But there were more and more occasions on which Keith began to appreciate our family as a complete unit and to acknowledge Bob's death as an accepted fact. His first-grade teacher related one such instance to me: one of his "sharing times" was supposed to be on "what my Daddy does." When Keith got up in front of his class, his teacher commented that she suddenly realized how he must feel. Keith simply said, "My Dad's dead, but my Mom makes up for him," and then proceeded to itemize our activities, and sat down just as everyone else had.

Keith and Craig began to attach themselves to older boys and grown men. The roughhousing they had had with Bob was now transferred to other men. Bob's friends who were also my friends were sensitive to this need. But there was still the problem of trying to get the boys to realize their limits. Sometimes it was an effort to get them to leave some of these people alone. At times I had to physically pull them off other people. The boys seemed to want to cling to anyone. They also grew closer together and were each more aware of where the other was.

Craig became so attached to Keith that he would ceaselessly ask, "Where's my brother?" He wanted to be confident of any new situation all the time. Craig did not seem to have the same separation fears about me as did Keith in the beginning. The period from the sixth to the ninth month seemed to be the crucial period for both of them. As we went through Craig's birthday, then Keith's, the boys moved into a phase of depression, talking, crying occasionally, and restlessness at night. Craig took to moving into Keith's bed. Keith got bothered by this after a while, and then Craig took to moving into my bed in the middle of the night.

The first night Craig was in my bed, I thought, this has got to stop now, and so I got up at least a dozen times that night moving him back. He seemed to be especially restless after the lights were out, the radio turned off, and the house became dark and quiet. I was afraid to close my bedroom door for fear that Craig might wander into a part of the house where he could hurt himself. I tried different tactics that had worked with Keith at the same age—a light in the bathroom, an all-night stereo station, a night light. These had some effect but after a while they all seemed to fail. Over a period of time he was not as persistent about security, and after a year, although he would still get into my bed, it was around four or five A.M. rather than the midnight of six months before.

It was particularly enlightening to me to hear the responses of other children to the news of Bob's death. Craig's friends were also checking out what this new word meant. His two nursery school car pool friends all the way down and all the way back would ask Craig, "Is your Daddy dead?" Craig would answer, "Yes." And sometimes they would echo back a taunting, "My Daddy's alive. He's here." At other times they would ask, "Where is your Daddy?" And Craig would answer, "My Daddy's not anywhere, he's dead." At times I tried to add a supportive comment, but each time I did all three of them in the back seat would indicate their displeasure at my interrupting their conversation.

Keith, being older and more articulate, was concerned about all the social ramifications because he realized they somehow affected his life. What were wills? Who wrote them? Did they have to be obeyed? Where was our money to come from now that there was no Daddy to work? How had I decided who would take care of him if I died? In my answers to his constant questioning I tried to stress those values which I deemed important: social fabric, planning, the bounds of community and caring. It was through my answers to his questions that I came to realize that communities are formed through activities which give significance to isolated events. Keith's observation of the responses of other adults corroborated this view of the social structure, how it was constructed, supported, and given its internal life. He saw the involvement of a community that lasted well beyond the week of the memorial service. He watched people ask about me, listened to my responses, and observed their responses to what I had to say. I became terribly aware of how my words were used by him. At times the burden became intolerable.

Then at times I had to catch myself so that I would not be doing my own grieving through my children, a trap it is much too easy to fall into. I realized that to grieve through the boys would do the same harm as to live through them. They healthily resisted my falling into that pattern as well as the attempts of others to grieve through them. Once, after an especially heavy and gushy experience, Keith exclaimed, "I wish you'd tell that lady to stop patting me on the head, saying 'poor little boy.' I'm not poor! And I'm not little!" At other times I was aware of

Keith's using Bob's death to get his own way, and I took this as a sign of the beginning of the integration and assimilation of Bob's death. When disciplined or feeling burdened by schoolwork he would sometimes start recounting to his teachers how he had lost "just everybody."

In the final analysis children reflect the values of the larger society. And I guess I should have been less surprised at the questions raised than at the delayed timing on their raising. It took about eight months for Keith to start asking for a "new Daddy." The first time this happened I really found it hard to take hold of myself. I came to regard this as a reflection of the quality of relationship that had existed between Bob and Keith. Part of Keith's emphasis on the "new Daddy" came from the first-grade emphasis on boy-girl relationships. The world around us revolves around the idea of the couple. Though Keith had not seen much television, he had seen enough to see romantic relationships in second-rate situation comedies ("I Dream of Jeannie," for example).

In their play with friends, the children had always taken family role models, so part of his interest in the matter of remarriage and a new family came from other children. Throughout the winter he asked about a new Daddy, the possibility of increasing the family, and so on. One way of dealing with this came accidently. On a Friday evening he saw a show titled "The Brady Bunch," a situation comedy based on the alliance between a widower who had three boys and a widow who had three girls. When I first saw the boys watching this show I was appalled. Then I realized it provided vicarious escape from their own situation. Some of the bad dreams occurred less frequently. There also seemed to be less verbal pressure on me to get a new Daddy.

Through all this and coexisting with all the growth and development were attempts to keep Bob's memory alive. The boys sensed my edginess as we neared the one-year anniversary of Bob's death. I thought I had been careful not to say anything, but on Palm Sunday morning Keith was coloring in the dining room and called out, "Mom, how do you spell nature?" "What are you doing?" I asked from the bedroom. "Making a nature book," came the answer from the dining room. Oh, I thought, that's nice. We spent a lot of time outdoors, hiking, walking, talking about nature, etc. "N-a-t-u-r-e." Silence. Then about five minutes later, Keith called, "Mom, how do you spell circus?" Came the exchange and the spelling, and then tiger, elephant, and other items found in a circus. At this point I was curious enough to walk into the dining room. Seeing "The Circus Book," I commented, "That's neat," and then opened the page to read: "I love you and Daddy when we went to the circus and saw the lions and tigers and elephants." I gulped, swallowed hard, picked up "The Nature Book" to read: "I love you and Daddy when . . ." I smiled weakly and deliberately walked out of the dining room back into my room to wipe my eyes. He's trying to keep Bob alive, I thought.

When the tulips began to bloom that next week, Keith seemed to be more intense in some of his responses. I wondered if he sensed the anniversary. He asked one day, "It's been about a year, hasn't it?" When I answered yes, he talked about the tulips last year when Daddy had died, how beautiful the garden had been, and how he wished Daddy could have seen it. We sat down together and talked about the year, how the community had been with us and felt for us, what it meant to have the tulips come up again, and what we had all shared together. Craig at this time started to cry about his Daddy being dead. I was not sure whether he remembered Bob at all.

We had a beautiful spring this year. And on one of the loveliest mornings, Craig came into my bed around six-thirty, looked at me plaintively, and said, "I want a Daddy." I could only say, "I know you do."

4

Beginnings

Is this what it will be like? I looked around the living room for what seemed like a split second after I shut the door the Monday night of the death. The sharp pain that had earlier penetrated my body was gone. Instead there was just a sick feeling in my stomach. I seemed to have only two levels of emotional response—one of adrenaline charging through my body to give me the energy to get through the week, the other of incredible tiredness and physical heaviness. I turned out the light. Only the shimmering porch light from across the street came in through the living room window. Somehow it seemed to take forever to get into my bedroom. The bed seemed so large. There would be no struggle for my half of the bed or the covers tonight. I think I slept soundly, perhaps the result of being so emotionally drained. In the morning, half-awake, just becoming aware of the beautiful early spring day and sunlight, I reached over. No Bob. No Bob! That wasn't a nightmare. That was real! Everything's not all right! Monday night came back hard and heavy. The boys! I had to talk to them! The bedroom seemed huge.

I have heard many widows and widowers say, "I don't know how I got through that week." Yet I seemed to have boundless energy. It seems that not only is there the ad-

renaline pumping through the system but there is the sur-
plus energy left over from not having to live with someone, not having to share, to give. The very nature of
marriage requires enormous amounts of energy. It takes
effort to live with a person, to share one's inmost self, to
grow and mature in this relationship. This effort and energy are central to the fabric of marriage. Perhaps a
"happy marriage" is simply one in which the hassles are
worth the results. The fact that I did not have to share,
give, make myself vulnerable to another human being on
a daily basis at that level of intimacy meant that there was
a great deal of unused energy.

But the initial physical responses to the death of a husband or a wife differ with the nature and circumstances of
the death. One young widow who had nursed her husband
through a long illness simply slept for a full day. Several
women have commented that they walked about as if in a
daze, not really cognizant of what was going on. Some of
them, though, when questioned later, could remember everything, down to the last detail. Some who do not remember anything, I suspect, are trying to block out what was a
very painful experience. One woman who had watched
her husband die a very painful death remembered absolutely nothing of her husband's final lapse and the week of
the funeral. Only after she had somewhat recovered from
her grief was she able to remember. Some people seem to
go into a state of shock, which may be merely the body's
attempt to deal with the emotional shock to the total
system.

Sometimes there are feelings of helplessness, especially
in women. Women who think of themselves as *wives*,
rather than as women who happen to be married, often
think of themselves as *widows* rather than as women whose
husbands have died. This kind of thinking drastically limits
the view one has of oneself. My impression has been that
women who have struggled for a sense of identity within

their marriages are better able to develop a sense of their own identity after their husband's death. People who know me personally often say that I have a "strong sense of identity," though I am never sure whether some of them mean I know who I am and what I am, or that I have an overblown view of myself. At any rate, my search for myself began during our married life, and not only was our marriage the better for it, but I was the better for it when Bob died.

Some of the literature on grief talks about the "stages of grief," how a person first feels X, then Y, and only then Z. But it seems more accurate to say that all these stages are intermingled, blended together, and indistinguishable one from the other while a person is experiencing them. There is an assertion of self-identity. There is that feeling of responsibility that others often call guilt. There are feelings of anger. There is the desire to strike out. There is passivity. There is acceptance.

As I look back, I think Bob and I had a basically solid marriage, that is, we viewed going through the hassles as worth it, and the times of sharing were a valued part of our life whether that sharing was joyful or painful. We were conscious of how we each were growing. People often say that in a marriage people grow apart. Rather, it seems that people simply grow. People cannot grow together because each person is an individual and needs a certain amount of breathing space around him or her, room to grow and mature.

The focus of our most serious conflict was the women's movement. The specific issue was a consciousness-raising group which included some women Bob felt uncomfortable about. "They might give you too many ideas." That was it. That last year of our marriage was the most meaningful because it forced us to probe more deeply into ourselves than we had ever done before. We had "bottomed out," as it were, and were beginning to communicate more

openly and in a more trusting fashion of the possible consequences. Some of our friends were aware of these struggles.

With commitment comes a feeling of responsibility,
whether that commitment is from the viewpoint of a
marriage, friendship, or professional relationship. Everyone needs to feel responsible—but only to a point. At
that point, people begin laying responsibility on other
people, and the widowed person is often the most vulnerable. "I ate dinner with your husband, and I didn't notice
anything wrong with him," said one. "Didn't you notice
anything?" Translated, that reads: Aren't you guilty of
some failing? Or it may mean: Tell me you didn't, so I
can feel clean about not having noticed anything either.
Or, "I always said you cooked too well." Translated, that
reads: I guess I should have told him not to eat that candy
bar he purchased while complaining he had to lose some
weight put on from your cooking. All this whirls around
in one's head on awakening the second morning after,
reaching again, stopping, thinking, realizing it's real. I
caught myself still half-awake saying Scarlett O'Hara's
famous phrase, "Well, tomorrow's another day," and then
thinking, how trite!

The feeling of responsibility seems to force one into
feeling guilty in many little ways: Why *didn't* I notice
anything different that morning? *Did* I in fact cook too
well? Was Bob's ordeal of babysitting the boys just two
days before the turning point? How did the struggle
within our marriage contribute to the situation, or did it?
How did I feel about the last year of our marriage? Would
I have done anything differently, "if only I had known"?
The food and cooking aspect of the guilt disappeared
quite early: The next Monday morning, in that half-
awake state, I looked over at the open closet door, saw
Bob's clothing there, and felt I almost saw Bob. Those
clothes simply must go, I thought. At breakfast I broached

the subject with the boys: "Remember how your Daddy and I always gave your old clothes to people who didn't have enough clothes?" I asked. "Since your Daddy is dead, don't you think he would have wanted us to give some of his clothes to people who don't have enough clothes?" Both agreed, though Keith wanted to keep his father's favorite shirt, jacket, and a few ties. Better clean out those pockets; I never could tell *what* he put in them. First pocket. A candy wrapper. Well, I wonder where he got *that* one. Second pocket of the same suit, another wrapper. Fourteen pockets and fourteen candy wrappers later I felt absolved. That took care of one kind and layer of guilt. More layers and kinds were to come later.

Late Tuesday night, after I had written out the format of the memorial service, we were all sitting down and talking. Nancy Jo looked at me and asked, "Joyce, would you have done it any differently?" referring to the past year. Some of the women who had been in our consciousness-raising group were there, and we talked about the year, what Bob had said, how he had dealt with our struggles, how I had handled Bob's responses. "I honestly don't know," I said. I still honestly don't know.

Grief is painfully paradoxical. At the very same time one is despairing and hopeful, consoling others and inconsolable, being honest and open and dark and secretive. All through that week I reached out to others, genuinely concerned about their acceptance of Bob's death. I remembered how shattered people had been when a young friend of mine had died six years before. I saw the same shattered looks and wanted so very much to say to them, "It's okay." At the very same time I was building up within myself an almost unscalable wall.

I felt myself go cold that week. I realized that one overly sentimental widow we had known behaved as she did in order to physically reach out to people. Bob and I had been very openly affectionate, touching, hugging. Wednesday morning in the kitchen I felt a chill. There were no warm arms to move into. My sister and her husband stayed at my place Wednesday night. In the middle of the night I could hear them. I felt the blood pulse through. I felt a dull throb heightening in intensity. Is this what it's going to be like?—I wanted so much to ask someone—but whom could I ask? I felt myself becoming irritable from the lack of touch and of warmth. By the end of the week I just wanted to be alone. I persuaded everyone to leave Saturday morning and sunk my knees into the damp earth of my garden. I wanted so much just to sink my whole body into it.

Saturday night I felt so cold. I felt it so necessary to throw myself into the reality of Bob's death. Armed with about six hours of sipping Scotch I sat myself down and wrote to all our friends in all parts of the country. "Bob died last Monday night . . ." I wrote. By the thirtieth note it was sinking in. Bob died last Monday night. An old friend came over very late and I used him just to get some warmth back into my body. Just someone to hold on to, to thrash against, to cry and scream out the grief. Then he said, "You've worked out a lot tonight, but what are you going to do when you really get the lonelies?" "I don't know," I managed to choke out, "I just don't know."

That Sunday morning the boys and I went to church. People embraced me from all over. Each hug, each embrace, each touch brought back some of the warmth into my body. During the service there was a period for the early Christian kiss of peace. Nancy Jo and I just clung to each other. I watched how others watched me. It seemed so important to give them all some meaning to this thing that had happened to us all. I only hoped that I could get some meaning out of it.

What seemed utterly incredible, though, was how soon I lost the sense of being married. Though still going through the sleeplessness, the tossing, the half-awake state, somehow I didn't "feel married." Mentally, I grabbed on to anything and everything that would sustain that feeling of being married. I was appalled at how quickly I started deciding in terms of "the three of us." Other men and women have related similar experiences. They, too, seemed to lose that sense of being married and struggled to feel married just as I did.

Some people, women especially, keep the memory of their dead husbands by insisting on being called Mrs. (husband's name) Jones. I had already come to terms with that before Bob died. I was not a Mrs. Robert—I was a Joyce. Joyce Phipps was my identity. Several people pointed out the noticeable social distinction between widowed and divorced women—"and you wouldn't want anyone to think you were divorced, would you?" I began to get irritated with department stores and the like, which were willing to bill me as "Mrs. Joyce" or even "Ms. Joyce" but insisted on putting "Mrs. Robert" on my charge plate.

Almost everything I did gained significance in terms of whether I had done it before with or without Bob. That first Sunday at church was very hard—several times I wanted to turn and just smile at Bob during a particularly meaningful part of the service, hold a hand during prayer, share the religious experiences. I found myself not watching the news on television late at night because there was no one to discuss it with. When I later went to visit my parents in College Park, Maryland, I drove through the University of Maryland campus and seemed to relive our courtship and dating days there. I also drove through Georgetown in Washington, D.C., but I simply could not take a walk there or go into the shops we had frequented or even sit in the park where we had always eaten our lunch. Since that first trip I have gone back to almost all "our places" and discovered that once the grief is worked through the memories are of a different quality. There is no longer pain but joy in being at those special places.

People around me tried very hard to help me in the assimilation of my grief, so that I could "start over," as one friend put it. They would not let me feel isolated. They seemed to understand the significance of special dates and made sure I had occasion to talk things out. My thirtieth birthday would come exactly one month after Bob's death, and Nancy Jo and her husband, together with the other assistant minister and his wife, planned a birthday party for me. Nancy Jo took my children out, helped them to select a birthday gift. Some of my neighbors came over. Another friend had remembered that our wedding anniversaries fell on the same date and invited the three of us over to her place. We were able to talk about our weddings—ten years before. The caring of the community was essential to my assimilation of Bob's death.

There were times I wanted to feel sorry for myself, but outside events were so overwhelming that my own grief seemed insignificant. I remembered Joe Hill's famous words, "Don't mourn, organize!" I felt the need to be into the world and to live in the world and contribute toward change—with a new desperation at times. I also began to hear of other widowed men and women who were far worse off than I was, so that any attempts at feeling sorry for myself became ludicrous.

The first time I walked back into the library science class I had been taking I felt my body grow tense. I did not know whether I would see that body, those faces, again. No one in the class said a word to me. At the break, everyone filed out. Only one student turned to me, plaintively said, "I'm sorry, Joyce. What more can I say?" "Nothing," was my reply. "Thanks for at least saying that." Left in the room alone, I turned and looked back to make sure there would be no body, no nurse, no ambulance atendants. There were none, and I could feel my body loosen up.

It's ironic, though, how the sharpness of the event crashes in on one when least expected. I had anticipated something in the library situation. Nothing. I tightened up at the first history department party. Nothing. But later I was yanked totally from the world of present experience and thrust into the world of painful confusion. On a sunny warm June afternoon during the annual college Children's Fair I was standing in front of the library and heard an ambulance tearing down the street. I was totally unprepared. I walked around as if in a daze for a few minutes. It seemed like that chilly April night all over again. One of my friends shook me by the arm, "Hey, are you okay?" "Yes, my God, that ambulance . . . a bit too much like . . ." "Okay, I understand," she replied. I was concerned that the next time would be in a situation that could have some tragic consequences, such as while driving, for example.

The nights were bad. There were times when I could hardly wait to get the children off to bed and "get some work done." I would stare at the house, go through Bob's papers, reorganize them, reshuffle, read his lecture notes, discard papers. Such busywork sustained me those first few weeks. It kept my hands and mind busy and at the same time forced confrontation with my memories. I, who previously had fallen asleep in the middle of my own sentences at ten o'clock, was now awake until two in the morning. A few nights I really felt tired, went to bed early, and awoke in the middle of the night. Sometimes when I awakened I would feel the coldness of the unshared bed, the dull throb in my body, at times heightening to such intensity as to almost be unbearable. The lonelies had arrived and I had no way of coping with them. I became a late-night movie addict so that I would be *so* tired that I simply would not awaken to the empty coldness.

I can remember commenting to a friend after seeing her kiss her husband good-bye that I envied that kind of touch, caress, and kiss. Being my age and candid, she asked, "I wondered how it would feel being cut off like that," with a downward stroke of her hand. "Hell, sheer hell," I answered. "What are you going to do about it?" she asked further. "I don't know yet," I went on, "maybe, just work so that I'm so exhausted that I can't think about it." "Oh," she laughed, "you certainly can *think* about it when you're utterly exhausted. You just don't have the energy to do anything about it."

I noticed that though people were willing to start talking about the boys "needing a father" or "you're young yet" or "you need someone to talk to," they were careful to avoid any discussion about the sexual dimensions of grief. In the year and a half since Bob's death I have realized the strong link between grieving and sexual need. I have broached the subject with many of my newly widowed friends, and much of the response is the same, "I thought I was abnormal, missing it so much." Many men and women have felt guilty about their needs. Some have done some dating a year or two afterward, defensively explaining, "We're just friends," afraid to open the whole area to self-scrutiny. One man, in describing his "affair" with a young widow, cried out, "I can hold her, kiss her, but I just can't . . . Oh, my God, I wish I felt free enough to really love her!" Another young widow told me of her affair with a married man, justifying it: "I can't marry because of Harry [the dead husband] and he can't marry because of his wife."

We seem so constrained that we cannot accept sexual responsiveness as a normal part of life. Perhaps we have been so trained to think of sexuality in terms of marriage that we cannot deal with the issues that sexuality raises after a marriage is ended. Society and the clergy especially are so tradition-bound that they are willing to suggest going to preposterous lengths to avoid heterosexual contact. One Roman Catholic widower told me that his confessor had told him to masturbate to relieve the physical tension from lack of sexual contact. As I began to look around to see how I would deal with my own tensions, I decided that I would try to handle them in a human way —in a giving way. I simply needed the opportunity to present itself.

There were times when the demands of those sexual needs were especially harrowing, the time an old friend of mine whom I had not seen for a long time gave me a big hug and I pulled back, visibly embarrassed because of the physical response I felt in my body. Fortunately, he and his wife, standing right next to him, a member of my consciousness-raising group, realized what had happened and understood. I did not have to make any apologies. I went through a period of trying to talk the miseries out with friends. I went through a period of going to singles' parties, but found everything so tedious that I withdrew in disgust.

I also misjudged some situations, but fortunately was able to extricate myself before I had regrets over words or actions, or both. Sexual word games between married couples are common, but when the word games begin between someone else's husband and oneself, then one begins to wonder. Some widows have commented to me that their married friends would not trust them alone with their husbands. But I wondered if these widowed people would trust themselves alone with their friends' husbands. One husband, persistent to the point beyond being chummy, found himself at a loss when I retorted to his "Come on, when will you take me seriously?" with a "When your wife tells me to." I became fearful of any kind of male contact for a while, as—I learned later—have other women in similar situations. One middle-aged widow I knew told me she went to every possible dance so she could overcome her fear of male contact. Dancing relieved some of her sexual tensions, but not all of them.

I also expected to have to deal with guilt and anger feelings. But my anger was not what I had expected it would be. At times I would be angry with Bob for not having taken the doctor seriously. At times I would be angry with myself for not having seen to it that he took the doctor seriously, but then I would sit back and remember that I had wanted room to move, to flex my intellectual muscles, as it were, to grow and make some independent decisions, and I realized that Bob had to have the same freedom I wanted for myself. I certainly didn't want to become a female chauvinist pig!

My anger stemmed mainly from my lack of patience with certain situations or with the people who created them. There was anger directed toward the Social Security administration because of the bureaucratic red tape I felt was unreasonable. There was the anger at friends because they were either hovering too much or did not seem to be listening. There was anger and resentment toward my parents, who seemed overanxious to remedy my widowed situation. There was anger toward my children because they did not seem sensitive enough at certain times. There was anger at myself for being angry.

The times I was most angry with myself were those times when I took out my frustrations on the children. I would lose my temper and shout at them when it was utterly unnecessary. Then, very often, I would cry and make up with them. I found myself expecting them to respond like adults; then I would catch myself, realizing, of course, that they could not respond but as children. Another widow, left with two young chldren, said she found herself resenting the fact that her children were alive and her husband was dead. She had not been able to take any joy in the birth of her second child because all she could see was a dying husband. At a group discussion, another young mother, who was bound up with very traditional values and outlooks, cried out, startled, "Don't you feel terribly guilty saying that?" "No!" came the defiant response. As I watched the young widow talk through, confront, and integrate her grief, her anger subsided.

The kinds of anger and guilt that are normally discussed "in the literature" seem to be reflections of that community of survivors which seeks out professional help. Guilt as a complex series of emotions is interwoven with the background, the circumstances of death, the supportive aspects of the community and family, the relationship with the dead husband or wife, and one's own identity. It seems that very often guilt is the term used as a catch-all; we narrow down all these threads to be able to articulate some of our feelings and emotions. The language of grief —like that of love—seems to be so limited. We who are grieving should form the language, invent the terms which apply to our emotions, rather than permitting other persons or communities to apply their terminology to our feelings. Perhaps one reason the psychiatric community sees so much of the grieving process manifesting itself in what is called "guilt" is because by the time most people get professional help they are beyond "normal grief." However, the distinctions that are often made between "normal grief" and "abnormal grief" seem artificial and arbitrary.

Many of the problems related to grief have little to do with the death itself. One widower, who discussed suicide as "another alternative" to living, stated that he felt "guilty" about his wife's automobile accident. This was compounded by a shattering faith crisis which he had been going through for some time. His first words to me three weeks after his wife's death were, "I don't know where she is. I wonder if she's hurting now . . . If only I could be sure about where she is now." It seems that his wife's death was the final alienation in a serious continuing loss of faith. Several others who said they experienced a great deal of guilt and anger confided that these feelings often had little to do with the actual death but rather with the circumstances in which they had been living. Bad marriages, lack of communication, frustration at work, extramarital affairs were determinants of "guilt" as well as the feelings of responsibility toward the now-dead person.

The week after Bob died a minister who had been aware of our struggles to open the lines of communication and widen the circle of tolerance stopped by to see me. He was sensitive enough not to use the word "guilty" either as a possibility or as a condition to be avoided. He asked simple, direct questions, and he let me be the first to introduce the word. "One friend asked me if I wouldn't change the last year over again," I told him, "but I strongly feel that the growing was so important to us both that I would not have changed anything. I think, if anything, I would have confronted Bob earlier had I known there was so little time left." As I thought back, yes, I wouldn't have waited so long, I wouldn't have been afraid of hurting him. That would have been distrustful of his ability to cope, to change, and to grow.

I asked myself some really probing questions: Had I wanted change? Or, had I wanted out? A number of times I had just looked around and thought, I want out! Out! But then one realizes there is no "out"—only some real change. I caught myself thinking the same thing after Bob died—out! I want out! A natural feeling, I thought. What counts is not feeling trapped. What counts is feeling that you can change what's around you. I really had wanted changes, I really did want our marriage to "work," our relationship to deepen and to grow. "If only" I had been more trustful of Bob's ability to change, to accept me as I had grown, then I would have confronted him earlier and our growing could have been more in tune earlier. "If only" he had confronted me, then perhaps some of the pain I had caused him could have been dealt with earlier.

But one doesn't live in a "perhaps" or an "if only" world. One lives in the world as it is. One uses the experience for more growing, better growing, more sharing and giving to others. So I learned not to put off painful confrontations because there is too little time to waste in not facing people directly.

5

The Outer Limits of Caring

My parents arrived Wednesday afternoon. My mother asked what she could do to help. I looked at her and said, "Nothing. It's all been done." Just then a friend, one of the women of our church, arrived with my laundry basket, every item ironed. My parents, understandably, looked startled. As I began to explain how all this had come about, another person arrived at the front door with our dinner for the evening. I sat down with my parents and tried to tell them what everyone had been doing. During this time about half a dozen people came in, each with something they thought I would need, each of them needing support through our common grief. I did not get a chance to fully relate all the happenings until late that evening, after eighty or more people had come in and gone out, each one offering help, talk, child-care, consolation to my parents, each one the member of some different community of which we had been a part.

As I thought about the relationship of "community" to the neighborhood in which I live, the town, and the metropolitan area, I remembered someone's observation that there is not one community, but layers of communities all interwoven as a piece of fabric, which is then cut into some sort of shape. There seem to be layers of communities even within the neighborhood. The people who live on my street, for example, represent different interests, political affiliations, religious denominations, educational backgrounds, and ethnic origins. Each one of these persons brings to the neighborhood some individual strand of the fabric and each person helps integrate those strands by participating in those events which he deems important or seeks to make important, such as a wedding or the death of one of the members of the neighborhood.

Most of us are searching for "community" or a "sense of belonging" which permits us to use the external structures of our communities to give significance to different events in our lives. Many of us miss this "community" because we expect it to function along certain preordained lines. However, to be in a community we must all participate in those activities which can be called community-building. When an event which is significant to one person's life is made to be communally significant, then there is communal feeling, though the focus is on the particular event.

After observing the community's responses to Bob's death and to my need for emotional support, my parents commented how nice it was to live in such a small community like the New Haven area (about a quarter of a million people), where, unlike Washington, D.C. (with about two-and-a-half million), people really cared for each other. Actually, the community had responded because Bob had responded to the community. Bob had become one of the arteries, pumping his life's blood, as it were, in the form of ideas, work, and money, into the various attempts of the communities to develop. The college community would miss him because he had become such a vibrant and important factor on campus, not only through the channels of college government and faculty politics but because he was open with the students as well. The church community and the political community would miss him for the same reasons. Bob had served as mediator and conciliator in all three communities.

Each community seemed to be aware of responding as a community. The neighborhood responded as a neighborhood. Each member of the neighborhood told someone else of the event. Everyone checked to make sure that other members knew and had made some external signal of sympathy. They constantly checked to make sure I was "not alone." The neighbors' concern extended far beyond the first week. One, a German World War II widow, came over one night and the two of us sat on the porch steps commiserating with each other. Another, with young children of her own, seemed to always have my children in her yard. A third would volunteer her children to keep an eye on mine if I had an errand to run or something important to do. The neighbors with whom we had spent the most time, arguing politics, sharing ideas, and drinking coffee, stressed repeatedly that *any* time I needed them they would be there. The wife, crossing strands of community, also served as a conduit of information in and out of one circle of political acquaintances, the local League of Women Voters.

The political community of which we were members tended to be quite disparate, as are most such groups, and its members tended to respond more on an individual basis than as a unit. However, the response touched more bases than I would have first considered possible. The network of information ran quite wide, spreading from those we knew in the New Haven area to people we had met once or twice who now lived elsewhere. Those immediately adjacent to us here filled the house, stuffed my refrigerator, reached out to my parents, and wrote notes to others we had known across the country. The letters came from all over, and I felt some sense of comfort would be given Bob's sister and my parents if they had a chance to read the cards and letters; so about two months afterward I sent them to Bob's sister, who then forwarded them to my parents. Community response was very important to all of us.

The college community responded both in its official capacity and as individual faculty and students. The presence of the college community was felt as early as Monday night, when the departmental chairman with several other faculty members came to the house. Tuesday saw the wife of the college president and faculty wives helping with the arrangements, the guests, and many of the small details that needed to be taken care of. Classes in the division were canceled the day of the memorial service. The college newspaper printed an "In Memoriam" edition, containing the "Thanksgiving for a Teacher" delivered by Bob's closest friend on campus.

In each of these communities there seemed to be one designated person through whom the information passed. One faculty wife spent two days on the phone telling other faculty wives what needed and what did not need to be done. One neighbor kept an eye on the house, sending over other neighbors so that I would have someone with me until my family arrived. The women's federation of my church put together the dinner that we would eat after our return trip from Brockton. As the wider community read of Bob's death, they called the people they considered to be the funnels through whom our needs would be made known.

These various communities gave because Bob had given. They cared because he had cared. By Tuesday evening, when I wrote the memorial service, I was beginning to realize the significance of what was occurring. I witnessed a grieving and sharing together by people who did not normally share very much; I also witnessed the tightening of some of those strands of community fabric. People from one kind of community were appreciating people from another kind. I wanted the memorial service to tie together all the seemingly fragmented elements of Bob's life, to show that, rather than being disparate, they were parts of a whole welded together. I chose biblical passages that would indicate the biblical foundations of Bob's activism, a hymn that would symbolize the historical side of his interests, a modern hymn that would manifest the contemporary understanding of the Bible and tradition, and three thanksgivings touching on the three main areas of his life. I planned the memorial service to be a community event—meaningful for each person's perception of Bob, as well as for each person's view of himself as a human being in this society.

The variety of individual responses as well as the depth of some of those responses was extraordinary. One good friend sat in the living room, utterly stunned, drinking fairly heavily. He reminded me of how Bob shrugged off concern about his weight. As I watched him, I thought of the young resident at the hospital who could not bring himself to say "He's dead." Others responded initially as I did, by keeping busy to relieve the physical tension. When I opened my door Wednesday morning, I faced six young women from my church who had come "to clean house." There was a zeal with which they literally attacked my house. One went to the store and did my errands. Another did my laundry. Still another did the ironing. Yet another vacuumed my living room. As I observed their efforts, I wondered what on earth had overcome them; but as I went through my own stage of compulsive working several weeks and months later, I appreciated the tension-release value of physical labor.

The initial responses of the students were equally overwhelming. I had known that Bob was a really good teacher (he had been my teacher in my college days). I knew the time and energy he had given his students, not only in school but bringing them home, counseling them, etc.

Those students, past and present, called, wrote, or tried in some way to express their grief. One person, a friend of one of Bob's former students, but who had never even sat in one of his classes herself, kept stuffing my refrigerator with food, "because you're going to have lots of people to feed." She kept checking on our needs up to several months afterward. Thursday morning, just before the memorial service, I took my sister and her husband to the college library to see the Tiffany windows Bob and another faculty member had extricated from our church basement and had persuaded the administration to mount on huge brass frames on the first floor of the library. As Keith and Craig raced about the library, I noticed not only that it was emptier than usual, but also that there was an audible sound of muffled weeping. I wanted so much to shout out some consolation to them all to say, "It's okay," but instead simply found myself squeezing shoulders and looking into their faces with a thanks for loving him, too. I later discovered that many classes had been canceled that morning to permit students to attend the memorial service.

The responses of church members covered the gamut. One woman, on her way out from the memorial service, looked at me, simply radiant, grabbed my hand, and said, "Joyce, you're a credit to your faith." I mumbled an embarrassed thanks, wondering what my "faith" had to do with my comportment. I thought about it, and I realized that her comment reflected the truth more than I had first appreciated. Her set of beliefs was poles apart from mine; in fact, the same woman had once questioned how I could call myself "Christian." But the attitude and mindset that provided the basis for my "beliefs" went deeper than even I first suspected. Both she and I recognized the validity of the religious experience even though the language used to describe it varied from person to person.

Several months after Bob died, several people commented on how well I looked. I was puzzled. How did they expect me to look? Haggard? Tired? At times such comments seemed to be asking: Tell me, how have *you* accepted his death? How have you dealt with your own mortality? At times the comment seemed to be: Look mournful! How dare you smile and laugh? At other times the comment was a questioning: Have you found peace?

One response that I had not expected was the desire to listen on the part of my friends, both close and casual. People who were asking questions were trying not to appear merely curious or morbid. There seemed to be a general attitude of disbelief concerning the whole situation. People seemed to want to verify the normalcy of their responses. For many of our friends in the same age group, this was the first direct contact with death as adults. Some of them had lost a grandparent; most of their parents were still living. Many I knew appeared to be asking for some explanation of the death, an explanation to offer their children, and some reference to Bob's role in their lives.

The Sunday after the memorial service all the churches in downtown New Haven had a joint worship service followed by a picnic on the Green. Members of other congregations greeted me, indicating their sense of grief by an embrace and extending their fellowship to me. The variety of response was immense. Some wondered how I had the "courage" to come to church; I could only reply that it would have been worse to stay at home, feeling sorry for myself, trying to tell my children we were not going to church because Daddy had died. One older widow came up to me and said, "You're young. You'll get over it." I started, thinking, how would she like it if I said, "You're older. You'll get over it." Then I recognized that it was her way of saying that it was important to look to the future and not the past.

One typical response was the deadly hush that fell when

I entered a room, as if I were the harbinger of tragedy. And then there were those people who simply could not say anything. One woman could not bring herself to come to the memorial service because she was still distressed at her father's death. Another, three weeks after the memorial service, cried in my arms, remembering her own dead husband's funeral four years before. I really empathized with these two women and with the others who tried to avoid me, the memorial service, or any mention of Bob's death.

Another aspect of the grief of some of our friends was their assumption that there should be no changes in the things that touched Bob's life—from the most mundane to the most profound. For example, when I repainted the living room late in August, it seemed desecration to some, and when I made Bob's study my study, shifting pictures, furniture, etc., it constituted, for some, the most severe form of "forgetting." Several friends said, "Why, things look different now," with that tone of voice that demands explanation. My response came to be, "Yes, this house belongs to the three of us and we make our own compromises in living." With one breath, they would talk optimistically of my future, and with the next, deplore any changes.

As time went on, I did not feel "forgotten." I felt it important to thank communities that had cared and to thank them as communities so that they would feel encouraged to reach out to others when needs arose. One Sunday, during the end of the "concerns of the church" period in the service, I thanked the congregation as a Christian community, and tried to convey my feeling that the community that functions along cohesive lines in times of grief would function along those cohesive lines at other times.

Occasionally I would meet people I had not seen since the day of the memorial service, and they would apologize for not having called. I knew that they thought of the three of us, or of Bob, and went on to assure them that lives do not stop because one man dies. I would then go on, saying that the best way anyone could mourn Bob would be to live life more fully, completely, and lovingly. Sometimes such a person would say, "I feel so guilty . . ." and I would wonder, does he or she really feel guilty, or simply feel that one is supposed to feel guilty? Guilty about what? Sometimes people seemed to be apologizing that their grief was not as deep as mine was presumed to be. My reply was to the effect that grief could not be measured in amounts, but that grief occurs from different perspectives. Each perspective is a reflection of the nature of the relationship. Nevertheless, I had to struggle to avoid trying to impose my perspective on others. One friend commented, "It's funny how often I've thought of Bob these past few weeks." I smiled, putting my arm around her, saying, "Yes . . . yes." But what I wanted to say was: What do you mean, funny? Of course, you've thought of Bob! He's dead! But I saved that for my room alone at night.

One startling result of Bob's death was the way in which I was now viewed by the various communities. I found that older members of my church did not dismiss me as easily as they had before. Had I gained some new maturity in their sight? The department in which I was enrolled at the college permitted me some exceptions from the rulebook. Was this sympathy? On the other hand, people seemed much more to the point, less roundabout in their relations, assuming, I suppose, that if I could survive Bob's death, I had strengthened my whole personality. There was a reaching out from others, tangible signs of "We really care about you." People often like to do things for others, and need an excuse. I was an excuse. Some of my friends would just drop in and make some outward visible sign of caring. They knew they needed to make no apologies; they were acting within a context that made caring and giving safe for them instead of making them vulnerable to rejection.

At each stage I felt it important to acknowledge the reaching out, the caring. As I thanked people, I started relating all the individual activities to the realm of community building. Many responded quite positively to the idea that their individual activities had community significance; it seemed to give their particular activities a kind of permanence, some intrinsic value. Traditionally, the widowed and the stranger have represented the most powerless members of a society. How we treat those to whom we are not beholden through family or clan ties has been considered to be one of the indicators of the level of civilization. The behavior of people indicates that they understand what it is they are doing when they reach out to the widowed and the stranger. They are reaching the outer limits of caring.

🌿 6

A Woman's Place

Several months after Bob died a friend asked me how the new liberated woman felt. I replied that I felt like the female eunuch, and laughed. But that was no laughing matter. Whether one feels "single" again, that is, in a sexual and social sense, depends on the person, on whether the person is male or female, whether or not there are children, etc. I felt that I had been sharing common ideals, goals, and understandings with another person through our marriage, though that did not constitute the substance of my being. Since my wifehood did not encompass the totality of my individual life, I did not expect that my widowhood could either. However, I discovered that my expectations and those of the world around me differed greatly.

I noticed that people tended to be freer with their advice than before Bob died. The ease with which breakfast-paper stock market players passed out their advice simply astounded me. Ignored were my repeated assertions that I had retained professionals who were trained in legal and financial matters. Normally, the response was: "But you don't have anyone to discuss these things with—you're all alone." Those instant brokers and lawyers had no way of knowing, of course, that I had been the person in our family to balance the checkbook and keep the financial records, and that, though we had always discussed our financial decisions together, I had been the one to work out the nitty-gritty of the family budget.

Early in July, loaded up and ready to leave the Cape after a week of camping with an old friend of mine, the car would not start. The boys were worried. "What's wrong, Ma?" Keith asked. "We can't go?" Craig puzzled. Fortunately, the camper in the next lot had a pair of cables. At home the next morning the car again would not start properly so I took it to the local service station. The owner looked at the car, then at me, and asked, "How long you keeping this car?" "Not long, I take it." "That's good," came his reply. So I went to the library, got the pertinent issues of *Consumer's Reports*, read that night and all weekend, and Monday morning went to a local car dealer.

When I walked into the showroom and looked at a subcompact wagon, a salesman ran over. "What can I do for you, honey?" he said. I bristled. "I'm in the market for a car, and I read the *Consumer's Reports* on the Colt. Could we take it for a test drive?" He looked at me, then answered, "Well, dearie, when your husband [I was still wearing my ring] is ready to buy a car, you can both come in and we'll take him for a drive."

I stared in disbelief. Then, slowly, because I did not want to say what I was really thinking, I told him that I had said *I* was buying the car, and if he did not care to take me for a test drive, I would see the sales manager. He got the keys and off we drove. When we returned I asked him various questions about the car, and satisfied that not only did I drive the Japanese imitation of the Japanese imitation of the Volkswagen but rode with the equivalent in salesmen, I thanked him very much for his trouble and started out the door. He called after me, "Will you be bringing your husband in when he makes a decision?"

"Look, friend, *I* am buying the car, not a husband," I snapped. "And I have made one decision already, which is that women shouldn't deal with boys!" I was simply shaking with rage. Then I looked down at my hand, saw the ring, and thought, must I remove my ring for my independence?

The people with whom I had done business before continued their relationships without question; however, as I began to move into new areas, such as building, I began to get questions about why I was doing the buying, and so forth. "Look, lady," said one lumber dealer, "you send your husband over and then we can be sure you get what you want." Keith piped up, "My Daddy's dead, and, besides, my Mom does all that stuff anyway." The salesman was abashed and rushed to fill my order, but with such an air of commiseration as to be condescending. The unwillingness of men to explain to women what they would explain to men exasperated me.

I had done a good deal of thinking about taking off my wedding ring. Part of the reason I hesitated was my reluctance to explain children tagging along with a woman without a ring. I realized I was really caught up in images, external appearances, rather than reality. Taking off the ring came about like cleaning out the closet: one day I could not stand "it" hanging on me. I made a clear decision about a week ahead to take off the ring a certain morning. That morning I started to pull it off. It caught at the knuckle. I struggled, wondered what the ring was telling me, pulled it off, laid it inside Bob's ring, looked at them, and then closed the jewelry case.

The feeling was strange. I felt an air of finality that I had not felt before. I was publicly saying, "Look, world. I am not married." That is very different from saying, "Look, world, I am a widow." Several times throughout the day I caught myself feeling the left hand, third finger. It felt strange to be bare. I had gotten a tan at the Cape, and the white band showed up. My sister-in-law had given me a birthstone ring for what would have been our tenth wedding anniversary because, as she put it, "you'll need something then." The ring had four stones: a ruby for Craig, an amethyst for Keith, and two emeralds for Bob and myself. I put it on my right hand. I decided that if I did not wear *the* ring on my left hand, then I would wear nothing there.

My initial discomfort at being a single woman with children soon ceased. I can remember the first time I took the children to a store without the "protection" of a wedding ring. I said to the saleslady, "My husband is dead" as if it were some sort of apology. Intellectually, I agreed with many of the stands of the women's movement, but internalizing them, agreeing with them deep down, was something else. Liberation, as it is called, or openness, as I would prefer to call it, comes gradually. The whole process involves a freeing not only of oneself, but of one's relationship to the world. And the process is not slow or steady; it is more like the way a new pilot lands a plane, with all the fits and bumps, smooth runs, then fits and bumps until the plane actually stops.

I made a deliberate effort to identify myself in terms of what I was doing rather than in terms of relationships. When asked what I did, I normally answered that I was a student rather than a widowed housewife with two children. I found myself replying in such a manner equally to men and women. I had already begun using "Ms." in any correspondence I had. Somehow, before Bob died, whether I was "Ms." or "Mrs." was not an issue. Afterward, however, when people would ask, "Miss or Mrs.?" I would respond defensively, "Ms." The process of changing my credit cards helped to bring me from a defensive Ms. to an open, well-okay, so-so Ms. I began by writing with the shipment of bills I paid about midsummer. Some businesses and firms stated their policy was one of using "Mrs." What took so long and was so hard was the realization that my identity was not wrapped up in my credit cards.

At school I really felt things were moving along fairly well. In one course, not one of the students had been in my previous semester's class. I was not being queried on how I "was doing." I was being accepted for myself. Then one day the professor started talking about Bob's relationship to me as if Bob were still alive. I felt a sick thud in my stomach. On the way out one woman commented, "Oh, I didn't know your husband was on the faculty here." She looked at me curiously. "My husband isn't on the faculty here anymore," I responded. "He's dead." Halfway to the parking lot, I thought, now why did I do that? She had looked so startled that I felt guilty. Guilt about wanting to be accepted on my own merits was wrapped up in the grief I was still experiencing. At home I was a mother with two children; here I was a student. Again I forced myself into situations in which I would have to relate as a single woman to the world outside.

As the fall came around, I sensed that in many ways I was becoming desperate for male company. Library school yielded the expected ten-to-one ratio of women to men. One day as I was talking with a friend, the assistant rector of one of the city churches, I mentioned the need to have some male company and my fear of those first encounters at the same time. He suggested I go to a "singles' club" which he assured me was low-key and respectable. This group had a "happy hour"—at a time inconvenient to me because of my class schedule and the children. They also held parties on a monthly basis. I promised him I would go to one and try it out. I wondered what to expect. Cocktail lounges were not exactly my habitat, but I mustered up some courage and brought a friend along because I was so anxious about going alone. That party proved to be pleasant but dull, and I found the women much more interesting than the men.

Generally, the parties seemed stiffer than the more relaxed open atmosphere of the cocktail lounge. One evening, after I had been to the place a few times, I walked in, saw some friends, and sat down at the bar to spend a half-hour before going to the Yale library to study. I really *felt* single, and I guess that message was transmitted. I never got to the library, but ended up spending a very interesting evening at another old New Haven bar with a pitcher of beer and an assistant prosecutor. By 10:30 I felt I really had to get home to bed, said I had to get up in the morning; and the assistant prosecutor, who had taken me from the first bar to the second, said he would walk me to the car. I felt the strange freezing sensation come on, and when he assumed an air of familiarity I really found myself in a quandry. Caught between a desire to see what would happen next and some inner sense of distrust, my behavior became fairly erratic and my answers to his questions even more vague than before. When I bristled at his arm around my shoulder, he laughed, "Now you wouldn't be hiding a husband on me, would you?" I thought, if you only knew. "No," I said, pulling away but slipping my arm around his, "I guess I've been in the books too long." That's safer, I thought. I wanted to keep this safe and distant.

I had long feared what would happen when a man made a serious advance. In this case I was confused as to whether it was the experience or the man I distrusted. I decided, though much later, it was the man. Real ambivalences stirred up in me. I realized that I was not just single in the sense of unmarried, but single in other senses, other understandings. Decision making had to be free, true, but could not be totally removed from my circumstances. I also realized that I needed to develop a sense of priorities in terms of my time and energy.

There were occasions when I consciously used my widowed status to get someone's attention. I used my widowhood to gain sounding boards. I craved, simply craved, adult conversation. When I would begin discussing the death, people would simply stop talking and listen for a while. I could get them to open up and respond thoughtfully. Each conversation became a catharsis. In each encounter, during each discussion, I was developing a greater sense of identity, realizing more and more that I could not forget what had happened but that I had to build upon past experience. Gradually I began to use this new type of experience as a base upon which to build a new identity.

Some other widowed women I have talked to found themselves using their widowed status as I had done. Others could not get beyond it. One woman, whose total sense of being had been wrapped up in her marriage, referred to herself as "Dom's widow"—twelve years after the event. I noticed that many women removed their wedding ring from the left hand and put it on the right hand. They wanted to be considered single but felt a tie to their dead husbands through the wearing of their ring. Many women would simply wear their engagement ring. I attempted to see if there were major age differences in behavioral patterns. The only major age split seemed to be around sixty-five or seventy. These older women generally kept their rings on their left hands. Younger women tended to divide. Other women used the birthstone rings, with the birthstones of their children, as substitute wedding rings. It was some fifteen months afterward, when asked if that ring with the four stones was a substitute wedding ring for me, that I removed mine. I realized that with four stones, representative of the old family situation, it had indeed become the substitute ring. Removing that ring had the same air of finality as removing the wedding ring.

Some widowed women refuse to move into traditional male areas such as house maintenance or yard work but hire neighborhood boys to do the work for them. Some of them feel very defensive about their femininity. One woman with a young child would not fix a toy because "daddies do that, not mommies." The child, looking at his broken toy, cried out, "But when will you get me a daddy to fix it?" Other widowed women, rather than resisting any attempt to be matched, plunge into a social scene that transcends the normal limits of belief. Some women simply cannot bring themselves to make decisions by themselves. They feel they need a man to do the deciding. Often there may be a decision-making transference to a brother or father or brother-in-law. One woman told me that her son paid all her bills, arranged for the house repairs, and then she wondered why she could not feel independent.

Some women display independence very quickly. The pace seems to be determined in part by social class, education, income, and occupation. One woman resented being called a widow; in her social life she implied she was divorced and that the husband was out of the state. Women who have professional lives of their own seem to make the adjustment more quickly than women who are totally home- and child-centered. But there are exceptions to these general patterns, too. Many of the women I have spoken to have been strongly opposed to the women's movement. Part of the opposition comes from a strange sense of ambivalence about how they ought to feel about their independence. One woman, who had had a very unhappy marriage, told me that it took her years before she could admit to relishing her independence, rejoicing in her own self, and welcoming all the interesting opportunities wthout a strange sense of guilt.

Men, since they are expected to have identities of their

own, seem to have less ambivalence about asserting their preferences, refusing to compromise, or leading their own lives. But many men are also caught up in marriages which consume the totality of their lives, and when those marriages end by death, they, too, are lost, confused, and disoriented. Oftentimes people who have not gone through the experiences of grieving comment that men have it more difficult because "they don't have children to keep them busy." Sometimes men, especially older men who are grandfathers, plunge themselves into their children's families. If there are no children, they seem to become aimless.

When the widower is younger there are other difficulties. One man told me he was expected back to work the day after his wife's funeral, and he had no idea who would care for his children. Another told me he was wife-hunting, but would not take a "women's libber," because he had learned how impossible it is to care for a house and children, and to work at an outside job. Another man has had ten housekeepers in two years because he expected each one to be like a mother to his children so he could go on being the distant father he had been before his wife died.

Men, though, do not tend to think of themselves as "widowers" in the same way that women identify themselves as "widows." A man is *first* an attorney, a college professor, a trucking dispatcher, a salesman, etc. Widowers were consumed with activities outside the home and marriage before, and these things they did and still do are the major shapers of their mindset. In a social and sexual sense they are theoretically freer than women. But few of them use their freedom to the limit. Several widowers in their late forties have admitted to frequenting singles' clubs simply for the sheer physical release they find in dancing.

When men do deny sexual preoccupation, it is probably because they want to appear to women as nonthreatening as possible. As a rule, however, men are more open about sexual questions than women. One told me that his married friends josh him about his weekends, which are spent looking at television and fishing. Plaintively, he said, "My God, I wish I could, but who's going to look at a forty-five-year-old with a pot belly?" Some are caught up in their own chauvinism. They seem to be afraid that they "cannot perform," that any attempt will jeopardize their virility. Some men who are caught up in the sexual standards of the age use means such as films, pornography, obscene jokes, and masturbation to deal with their sexual frustrations. I have encountered very few women who will admit to masturbation, but quite a few men are open about it as a means of physical release. Some have felt there is more religious sanction for masturbation than for heterosexual intimacy. One area which seems to be a forbidden topic is homosexuality. This seems to be the ultimate threat to virility or to femininity.

There seem to be stages to how people feel about their singleness, though there does not seem to be any progression of stages, one neatly following the other. Concurrent with the ambivalence toward independence, and perhaps part of the reason for the ambivalence, is the feeling of not having to worry about what the other person will think or say or do. There is a sense that you make a decision to do something and then you do it. About the middle of August, after a week in a church camp, I felt depressed coming back to the house. I remembered what someone had said about a divorced friend feeling that she had to make the living place *hers*. It suddenly struck me that the whole house was a compromise, as it had to be for us to survive. I looked at the walls, the location of prints, the furniture arrangement. That same day I went to the paint shop. I chose a new wall, new woodwork. I rearranged the furniture and prints. The living room became *my* living room. I moved everything around in what had been Bob's study, and I made it *my* study.

I also had a strong urge to tidy up, to complete unfinished business. I had planned to donate the bulk of Bob's history collection to the college library, so I let many of Bob's friends go through the collection first. Some of Bob's colleagues asked me about Bob's dissertation. I told them I planned to clean it up and have it published. One of his colleagues cautioned me against living in Bob's shadow. I told him that yes, it was the easiest thing to do. At times I caught myself in that frame of mind. I realized how difficult it would be to create my own place in the world, not just from a social point of view, but from my own perspective as well. I have in the course of the past year and a half met more than a few women who have built their lives alone by living in the shadows of their dead husbands. That's where the pressure is, societally.

"You're young yet," commented one widow of sixty, "you'll remarry, begin again." I looked at her. Does beginning again mean that I must remarry? Are my options that closed? I told her I felt I was already beginning again, that even though I spent a good deal of time tying up loose ends, I had ideas about myself, my future, the children, and their futures, that my beginning again is as a single woman. Many of the widowed, because they have "traveled that road," as one woman put it, were very frank in their comments in areas where nonwidowed friends were vague and indirect. "You can't be alone at 3:00 A.M. for the rest of your life," boldly stated this same sixty-year-old. "No," I responded, "I don't intend to be, but I have to balance my sense of personhood against marriage. If I remarry it will be because I grow to love someone and want to marry him, not because I feel other options are closed to me." I studied her face. What does *she* do, I wondered. "I envy you," she continued, "you're young. You can change your thinking. I can't. I want a man. I want some love, but I can't bring myself to do anything about it outside of a marriage. I wish I were young enough to change some of my old-fashioned thinking. I wish I could respect myself and get some love."

Her voice was so moanful. I really felt for her. Her confusion reflects a good deal of the confusion I have seen, especially in those over fifty, but in many younger men and women as well. So emotionally committed have they been to the traditional views on marriage, sexuality, and love, that they cannot emotionally settle for a new mentality, let alone a new morality to reflect their new situation. Women, especially, feel that to begin again is to remarry, though there are quite a few who do not feel that way. Among some women there is a recognition of the need for change, adjustment, new opportunities. Women in the middle years, between forty-five and fifty-five, seem to be the most accepting of their new independence, and they seem to be relishing it the most. Most of the younger women are still too engaged in raising their children to feel any sense of independence; in fact, they seem to be the most overburdened.

As I struggled with my sense of myself, what I was to do, I "changed." "You're so different," friends would say. "Did you expect me to stay the same?" I would answer. The way in which many of my friends talked about what they perceived as major changes implied that they thought these changes would not have taken place if Bob were still alive. Of course, I would reply, people change as they are shaped by the world around them. I felt that had there been no change, no growing, then it would have been a comment on my insensitivity to my surroundings and to events. I had been changing and growing all the ten years of our marriage, and there had not been as much comment about it as there had been in the past year and a half. Much of this, of course, was due to the fact that Bob's colleagues, their wives, and the communities surrounding us all did not see me or the children as frequently as they had before. When an outsider doesn't see a child for a long time, he notices the growth that a parent is unaware of.

At times I found myself being forced into a niche by Bob's friends and colleagues. One old friend of his was startled when he came into what had been Bob's study. "You've changed it," he said with a "how dare you" attitude. His comment applied to me as well. I was Bob's wife in his mind. I had to fit all those images of what he expected Bob's wife to be like. Another commented, with emphasis, on how *well* I looked, as if I should appear in a constant state of agitation. I resented those remarks. They seemed to be saying, "Show your grief!" People seemed to be afraid I might "get over it," and I sensed their uneasiness about their own mortality. "Does it still hurt?" asked one, and I answered that, yes, if that meant did I still feel alone, apart, not having that level of intimacy with another human being that I had so treasured for almost ten years. But, no, it did not hurt in the sense that I could not remember with fondness and pleasure our good times, rejoice in the love that had been and be willing to risk again, be willing to endure the pain of grieving again. At times I sense bewilderment; at other times, open hostility; sometimes, understanding.

I did not feel that I was "beginning again," but continuing. I tried to take each new experience as something to build upon, to deepen my understanding of myself. There were ways in which I was just discovering myself. Occasionally I would amaze myself with an insight of or gesture toward someone to whom I had no previous commitment. I listened to men and women seeking out their own selves, gleaning as best I could what would and could apply to me.

7

Come Home

In a way, I knew my Dad had to say it: "If you ever want to come home, you're welcome." And my response was just as necessary: "I am home." I winced as I said it, and my parents winced as they received it. I knew that my Dad would feel it necessary to make that gesture. Letters had expressed the concern of loving parents. They were concerned about my financial status, the boys, and most of all, me. As I read them I remembered how my parents had been desperately searching for an excuse to go to the grocery store that first week after Bob had died, and when they finally found one they came back laden down with groceries. By early summer they were expressing other concerns. They asked how I was faring, how the boys were handling Bob's not being there, where all the pictures of Bob were (they were afraid that unless there were photos the boys would "forget"), and tentatively opened up other areas for discussion. I selectively told them of my talks with the boys and their emotional responses. I realized somehow they were not ready to hear what I was bursting to say. As they continued talking, I began to sense that they had a different view of me than I had of myself.

They seemed to be reassuming their former parental role, as if they had handed over custodial care to Bob and now that he was gone, they had to take over. They passed out advice on trivia and subjects of monumental importance with equanimity as if I were sixteen again. At first I thought their main concern was financial, so I explained all about the insurance policies, my financial security, and my plans. But as I eyed their responses, I realized that what they were expressing verbally was but a symptom of a much deeper concern. I talked about the new life I was leading; they were uneasy. I discussed jobs in Connecticut; they asked me when I would return to Washington. I found myself resorting not to deception but to reasons that I knew would satisfy them. When pressed on "coming home," I kept insisting that I was home, until I realized that I could get much further if I discussed staying in Connecticut in terms of the boys' security, the communities of which we were a part, small town versus big city, safe streets versus crime, and so forth. These were but outward manifestations of my instinct for remaining in Connecticut and creating a life for myself. After a really intense four- to six-hour discussion, my father concluded that I was probably right "for the time being" since all my friends were around me and I was so deeply involved with the church. "Besides, maybe the minister can find you a new husband."

I was flabbergasted. I just looked at them in disbelief. One part of me was thinking wildly, it's been less than three months and here they are already thinking of my getting married. Another part of me was ready to burst: I don't need a husband to take care of me! At thirty I could hardly be considered a child. All kinds of contradicting thoughts and feelings welled up in me. Part of me was hurt because I felt I could take care of myself. But my outward appearance and verbal responses did not reflect how I was feeling inside. I smiled, and said that, yes, friends were watching for me, and I was sure that if any likely prospects came along, the minister would be only too happy to pass him on to me. "You do want to remarry, don't you?" they asked uneasily, as if I would give the wrong answer. "It's too soon," I rejoindered. I felt dishonest in my responses to them, but I felt the need to terminate the discussion.

In August I felt it necessary to go south again to visit my parents, and to have the children experience their grandparents. Bob and I had usually driven at night, leaving about three in the morning and arriving before nine because then the children were asleep and less troublesome. We would bed down early and begin fresh. I told my parents I would be there by eight in the morning. They misunderstood, thinking I would be leaving New Haven at eight. But, on schedule, early Sunday morning, we arrived. They were visibly distressed: "What if—" I assured them that it was safer on a patrolled turnpike with only good truck drivers than it was during any normal rush hour. My parents could only go through imaginings of what would happen if—"If what?" I asked, clearly annoyed.

After a period of three days they brought up the question of remarriage again. I avoided discussing any of this as much as I could. Finally: "Do you still miss Bob?" my Dad asked. "Miss." There was a word. What did it mean? I told them that yes, I did. They then went through a whole range of issues they wanted to raise with me. "Don't get too independent." "You have to be more feminine." It sounded like high school all over again. After the lecture on how I simply had to get married again, and soon, and my protestations that I was doing just fine and that if the options opened up, then fine, but if not . . . my father came in on a different tack, "The boys need a father." I froze, furious. "Well, let them marry one, then!" I felt terrible afterward.

I turned all the questions over in my mind: remarriage just for a "father"? A person doesn't husband-hunt the way she house-hunts. I was ready for a few other sacrifices but not for that kind of commitment to anyone. I wanted an independent, self-directed life. I was not going to rush into any situation. I had not had any other male-related experiences yet. Calmly, I talked about married lifestyles, said that most my friends were couples, single men were hard to find, we had to wait a while, and that I had not yet worked through my own grief. I found myself making excuses to avoid questions and uncomfortable situations. My responses to that kind of parental concern, which becomes intrusion, were similar, I found, to those that twenty-one-year-old "potential spinsters" were forced to make to their parents.

Some widowed persons are very accepting when parents direct their affairs. Some either move into the parents' home or have the parents move in with the family. This seems to be more the case if the parent is a widowed person or if the young widowed person has children. One woman, who made this decision reluctantly, felt the need for the grandmother to care for the children while she worked. Another, a young woman without children, felt her mother needed help with the teenage children still at home. A third woman set up joint housekeeping in a new home because she "just felt more comfortable with Mother." One young man struck a bargain with his mother, in leaving his younger child with her during the entire week while he worked and supplemented her income. Another, a young woman who was clearly and openly looking for a husband, used her mother as a convenient babysitter while she went about her search. These sorts of situations, though, generally turn out to be very uncomfortable for all the parties involved. Mother is either there when the woman brings her date home, or disciplines the grandchildren differently, or trades her commitment for another kind from the child.

An entirely different perspective on this whole situation

comes with the realization that what you hear your parents saying to you at thirty is the same thing that others at thirty are saying to their parents in their sixties. I remember once turning to a middle-aged woman and asking her for some insight on dealing with people of her age group. She looked at me, smiled, and said, "I was going to ask the same question of you." When I asked her what she meant, she talked of her children saying to her, "But, Mother, you can't possibly manage alone." Her children wanted her to "come home," too. They had raised many of the same questions that my parents had raised with me: living alone, remarriage, new beginnings. Well, well, I thought, is this that common? As I began listening to more and more people, I found that it was all too common.

One wonders whether those comments, questions, and what sounds like constant nagging are really intended to be intrusions, or whether they are manifestations of something deeper. People need to feel needed. They need to know that their advice, support, and being there, really count for something in someone else's life so their efforts at being helpful are often tinged with a desperation that makes them heavy-handed and interfering.

So often I have heard a widowed person say to me, "But I can't just unload." Often, widowed people, myself included, have not really opened up the depth of their grief to parents, children, and other family members. The reasons are as varied as the people. Some parents, although they try to be useful in often intrusive ways, do not welcome such openness, which is what is really necessary. This is especially so if both are still alive, because the manifestations of grief constitute experiences they will someday go through. Some elderly people really feel uncomfortable with the ways in which a much younger person is grieving, and simply cannot relate to those feelings. Some parents simply cannot bear to see their children in such pain.

One young woman talked about her family's refusal to discuss her husband's death "because of the children." They talked about family life as if the husband had never been there, refusing to accept any changes in the children's behavior, and removed all his pictures from their living room. The opposite reaction also occurs. Pictures put up as densely as votive candles in a chapel, constant discussion with great profusion of tears, telling the children how much they (the children) miss their father, "but never mind," with hankies and sniffles, "he's gone to a better world." This mother finally refused to take her children to her parents' home until they realized that this kind of behavior was interfering with the life she was trying to build with her children.

And when there are parents-in-law the situation can become even more complicated. One woman told me how two months after her husband's funeral, her parents and parents-in-law had left her house following a violent argument. The widow's mother had told the husband's mother how she hoped her daughter would remarry. The mother of the dead man was stunned, and verbally hit back, and, in her still-intense grief over burying her son, threatened all sorts of havoc if this young woman (in her mid-twenties) ever, ever remarried. Another woman, also in her mid-twenties, found herself in a very awkward situation when her young son, just three, announced to his paternal grandmother that "Mommy's going to get us a new Daddy." Of course, not all parents try to foist marriage onto their children. Just as frequently the attitude is, "You've been married once. That's enough," delivered in a tone of voice to suggest, "You had your chance in life and muffed it."

Some people have attributed these parental attitudes to the ethnic backgrounds. One woman, Irish, spoke of a common Irish attitude. Another, Italian, said it was peculiar to Italian culture. Another decided it was New England Puritanism.

Sometimes parents have been so destructive of their children's attempts at searching themselves out that they opposed remarriage wtih a view to tying the child to themselves. But probably just as often, children cling to their widowed parents in exactly the same way. Someone has observed that for parents to "let go" of their children, children must "let go" of their parents, too.

There do exist rare parents who resist the attempts of their widowed children to hold on to them. One older woman bemoaned her daughter's lack of independence: "John was her whole life. She never had a life of her own. Now she needs someone to take care of. Well, it won't be me." A rather intense personal struggle ensued for several years until the younger widowed daughter remarried. "She has someone else to occupy her time now," the mother happily reported. "I just hope that I pass on before her second husband does. Next time I might not be as strong."

Some parents of widowed persons are fully aware that their children are taking advantage of them but feel bound by parental duty to let them do so, sometimes to the point of mutual disaster. A couple now in their retirement have become surrogate parents to their grandchildren; others have given a great deal in financial support when it was not needed; still others have given up their own independence to move in with the widowed child "to help out." "What else could I do?" is a common response in such cases. "I just couldn't say no." Some of the children are aware that they are using their parents; but most would not acknowledge that they are taking advantage of their parents.

Many of these attitudes stem from the fact that in a mobile society we are still trapped by archaic notions about the roles of parents and children. A good many people carry a fair amount of guilt because they can talk better to their friends than their family, because they feel more comfortable needing their friends than their family, and because they would rather live in the environment they personally have created. After a relationship has been built through a marriage, many ties with parents and the original home environment will certainly be broken, in some cases physically by distance, or else by social and cultural differences through education and occupation. And although knots can be retied, they can never be retied in exactly the same way. Whether a marriage has lasted six months or sixty years, there will have been fresh perspectives gained, new responsibilities assumed, and new relationships created.

One man told me: "I know that I ought to feel closest to my Mom and to Betty's mother, but I can't talk to them. They don't know how I feel." He went on to explain that he could talk out certain problems with his friends, and with someone else who had been widowed as well—though he had not known this person until his own wife died. His widowed mother and mother-in-law "belong to another generation, you know." This example is not unusual. Even without class differences, educational differences, and financial differences, the sheer changes in society and the age differences preclude the possibility of open communication. Though the parent can let go of the child, and the child of the parent, rarely it seems is it possible for one to be able to see the world through the eyes of the other.

These perception problems are compounded by language problems. Around Christmas my father asked me, "Do you still miss Bob?" I replied that I did because it seemed like the best answer to a vague question. As I watched his response, I thought, he means, am I still grieving, or have I "gotten over it" sufficiently to start husband-hunting. Then I mentally rapped my knuckles at being so insensitive to my parents' concerns and needs. Parents often feel more experienced than their children, and children, on the other hand, often feel that they are more in the "real world" than are their parents. When I first thought of returning to Washington, I feared the consequences of the religious, social, and political differences with my parents. My children experienced such differences as well, in terms not only of their grandparents but of the different community. During the summer, Keith was fascinated by all the talk of bussing in the county school system. Talking to one of my parents' more racist neighbors, he said simply, "Well, if you don't want to ride busses, and you gotta go to school with brown [his word for black] children, why don't you all just live in the same neighborhood?" He was genuinely puzzled by the woman's reply. The great difficulty of living *my* life in the same geographic area as my parents seemed to be balanced against the great difficulty of creating an independent life in my own metropolitan area.

At first I thought in terms of the individual clashes of social and political attitudes. Then I began to look at the ways in which my parents related to my children. After each visit to Washington I would hear my children talk about how much they would like to live closer to their grandparents. One day Keith broke into a conversation telling me breathlessly how lucky a schoolmate of his was: "His grandma and grandpa live with him. He gets to see them every day!" When questioned as to how this friend of his liked having his grandparents in the same household, Keith said, clearly puzzled, "He doesn't like it. He says they're just like moms. Isn't that silly? Grandmas aren't like moms." And as I observed the close-knit ethnic families around me, I began to wonder if the role of the grandparent, as I appreciated it, was sacrificed where the grandparents became totally responsible for the grandchildren at an early age, where they were not indulgent. I remembered my preschool childhood, how around Craig's age I had been given the special treat of walking down Wilson Street, down the narrow steps to the street below, then down to Rollstone Street, to get an ice cream cone with my grandpa. Those trips were a special part of my childhood. I was aware how trips to Grandma's and Grandpa's had already become special and exciting and something to look forward to for Keith and Craig. I became concerned that the specialness might not be lost only for the children but for the grandparents as well. "Coming home" would put added burdens on them, as well as upon me. It seemed that it was important for grandparents to remain grandparents and not become surrogate parents.

Beyond those considerations I also wanted to be sure that pressures put on me would be of my own choosing. I wanted to be free of the social pressures to develop relationships with men or to not be too independent. I felt the need to structure my own life, respond to the needs around me, and to be optimally responsive to those needs. I acquired a "what they don't know won't hurt them" attitude, not very trusting, I admit, but what I began to feel a need for that first year was survival. I was sure that if I could make it through the first year, then I could manage for the future.

The more I felt that my anwsers put my parents off, the less defensive I became. I grew more willing to say what I was really thinking rather than what they hoped I was thinking. By the Christmas trip I was ready to make very clear that I would probably not return to Washington unless there were some major change, such as a job too good to turn down. Christmas was a turning point in many ways. Five minutes after I arrived I was informed that I had a date for that evening. I tried to be nonplused but I was clearly shaken and remained shaking until my sister arrived with our escorts for the evening. My parents looked him over in such a way as to be embarrassing. The next morning my mom asked me what time I got in. I was taken aback. Again I felt treated like a child.

They were somewhat upset that this had been my "first date," but again I emphasized that I did not know single men. I had plenty of time, and besides, I was not so sure if men were worth the trouble. I became more and more open about my own ideas of my future. They were clearly pleased that the date wanted another date, and this time without the sister. My parents were ready to jump too quickly, I felt. Maybe I misinterpreted their responses. When I returned in February I was even more open than before and began to chance open arguments over my ideas of my own and the boys' futures. When they asked about my friend, I commented that I did not care for his racial attitudes. My father gasped, as if to say, you mean you threw away a chance because the man had prejudices? He said, "What's politics got to do with it?" "Everything," I replied, "e-v-e-r-y-t-h-i-n-g!"

As the discussions got around to just how did I feel toward men who did not agree with my political opinions, I tried to point out that there were certain fundamental differences between "political" opinions and life orientations, such as attitudes toward race. Anyone that I would be interested in would have to agree with me in certain fundamental attitudes, for example, that one accepts people as persons, not as races. My mother, clearly uncomfortable, shifted the topic, "Are you seeing men?" "Yes," I answered, "all the time," knowing full well what she meant. I did not feel that I was lying, but merely telling the truth in a literal sense.

Between visits I talked over common problems with others who felt surrounded if not threatened by their parents. One older woman, who had been widowed and then divorced from her second husband, cautioned, "Don't let anyone push you into anything. I let them push me into a disastrous marriage." As we exchanged stories of our parents and our children, we laughed. One young woman, who had been resisting the weekend matching games of her parents, said, "You know, if I took my parents seriously and did what they wanted me to, not only would I be a nervous wreck, but I'd be alternating between nymphomania and celibacy." An older woman told me of her daughter's response to her going for a ski weekend with a widower about her age. The daughter was shocked. "Now, you would think she would know better," continued this woman. "Everything was dutch treat."

A few widowed people really do want the guidance of their parents or children. They have been away from social activity too long to feel comfortable, and need the support their parents or children can give. Almost all experience the gamut of parental or child responses through the first year after the spouse dies. There is no such thing as a static situation. Attitudes, actions, and beliefs do change. Relationships continue to develop between parent and child. Part of the early strain comes from dealing with the grieving of people with different perspectives. As the multiple perspectives of sisters, brothers, sisters- and brothers-in-law, as well as a host of others, begin to come down on the head of the widowed person, life can become very confusing. Survival may become a game of manipulating one set of relatives against another. As one person told me, "Am I ever glad we live in a fast-paced, highly mobile society. I can visit them. They can all visit me. But I'm not stuck with living with them."

This past trip to Washington was the easiest of the lot. I felt open and nondeceptive in my answers and nonevasive in discussing my lifestyle. I talked about my plans with equanimity, and my parents seemed to accept my view of myself as a person who can chart her own course. People really can let others know where they are internally by their whole view of the world and the way in which they treat others. I was developing to the point at which I felt peace, inner acceptance not only of Bob's death but of the positive value it had contributed to my life and to that of my children. Communication with my parents was more direct now. The mood was more relaxed. To be sure, there are still lapses on both our parts. A letter from my Dad just a few weeks ago went about telling me how to be a librarian in typical Dad fashion. But I was not rankled. I accepted it for what it was—parental love and concern for my welfare and the need to feel helpful. Coming home I took the Merritt Parkway into New Haven. The view over the crest facing West Rock was breathtaking. I felt relieved. I had survived another trip. Only five more minutes through part of the city, and then I would, indeed, be home. The boys would be able to get out and run and tell everyone what we did for three days in Washington. I would walk into the kitchen, which would seem small by comparison to my mother's, make myself a pot of coffee, sit down, catch up on the mail, listen to the sounds, look about at the sights, sense the smells of home, and go and do the laundry.

8

The Business
That God Has Given

At a church program one of the ministers turned to me and asked how I was doing. As I started to talk to him about the three weeks since Bob's death, I suddenly became aware that everyone in the room was silent, seemingly transfixed. I looked about the room. I knew almost everyone there. I went on to describe what I had said to my children, how they were responding to the sense of community feeling and support. I noticed that both clergy and laity had the same hollow expressions on their faces; both seemed to be groping toward their own understanding of death. I then asked one clergyman how he would have dealt with the children. "I wish I knew," he responded. "I can't even deal with myself." I thought of my closest friend, on whom I heavily relied, who had not approached "comfort" with the "Now, there, everything's going to be all right" mentality, but with the realization that grief hurt and that the pain was necessary along with the grappling with fundamentals. She also did not face grief as a "professional," but as an equal who was grieving as well. She was a decided contrast to most of the clergy I encountered.

The cleric to whom my heart went out the most was a divinity school student just about my age who simply could not handle death. At first I had thought him an exception because he had lost his own father at age seven. I soon discovered that most of the clergy had severe problems facing death themselves—problems which they transmitted to the people they were counseling.

Over the first few weeks I found myself "comforting"— if that is the word to use—the clergy, and soon found myself wondering what it was that they had "learned" or at least discussed in divinity schools. As the first summer progressed and I came into contact with more and more ministers, I was literally appalled at the unwillingness of the clergy to deal seriously with death. I could only remember hearing two sermons on death—one during Easter almost ten years ago in Washington, D.C., and the other as a Christmas sermon by William Sloane Coffin in which he described the death of his uncle, Henry Sloane Coffin. Every Easter there was, of course, the traditional pap about how though Jesus suffered death on the cross, he rose, etc., so that the death was of no consequence.

Of no consequence! Death as I met it was pain. Some esoteric idea about pie-in-the-sky did not help the fact that Bob was gone. A belief in the immortality of the soul did not erase the loneliness I felt and still feel when I walk into the house. When I open the door, there may be a cat or two, but there is no Bob. And when I wake in the middle of the night, my bed half-empty, cerebral meditations on the resurrection and the life to come remain cerebral. The talk that Daddy may be an angel flying around or one of "God's helpers" does not compensate for there being no Dad. Grief is often treated as a condition to "get over," a sort of understandable aberration from the normal.

I realize how very fortunate I was in having had some clergy around me who were sensitive. The number of evenings I occupied in seemingly endless talk on a combination of significant and trivial subjects are beyond counting. I did not hear too much from the "buck up, old girl" school, but most of the bereaved persons I have spoken to over the past year and a half have received just that kind of response, coupled with helplessness concerning the questions of children and an almost complete avoidance of the whole area of sexuality and identity.

A good deal of the failure of the clergy is a reflection of the society in which they live. Divinity school training, for example, does not on the whole grapple seriously with many of the issues raised by grief. For most clergy, the demands of their day-to-day parish activities simply do not allow them the time required for follow-up on any one particular bereaved person. There is also the temptation to assume that a person in grief who needs help, advice, or just moral support for what he is doing will *ask* the clergy to provide such. Many of the clergy respond just like "ordinary" people, who presume that once the grieving party has stopped looking as haggard as before or has begun to re-enter the world in no matter how automated a fashion, the grief is ended. However, sometimes the clergy meet the grief head-on when symptoms appear as other kinds of problems in areas such as remarriage, handling difficult children, depression, etc.

It seems that so many of our church problems with death are rooted in the traditional Christian perspective toward death. "Now, Mummy's gone to heaven," said one father to his child, and the minister standing by confirmed his story. Yet the children witnessed all the psychological shocks of separation and grief in their parent. "If heaven's such a grand place, why is everyone crying?" asked a five-year-old. A quick-thinking Sunday School teacher answered that it was because we would not see that person for a very, very long time. But that child, at five, had no conception of time. "At least not for a whole hour?" Historically, from a theological perspective, this earthly life is supposed to be a preparation for the eternal life to come. There have been cultures that accepted this idea in their grief; for example, the ancient Greeks celebrated the departure with a banquet. This sort of thinking has been carried into our own day; in the Church of England and in Roman Catholicism, for instance, the mourning color can be white to celebrate the entrance of a soul into heaven. But theological celebration, on the one hand, and grief, on the other, give rise to ambivalence and confusion. Many clergy today have not resolved their own ambivalent feelings toward death. In a time of grief, they seem to fear that the ambivalences will become pronounced, so to appear "consoling" they deliver only clichés. The point of this kind of consolation is to try to convince the bereaved that they should get over their grief as soon as possible so they can stop upsetting the world around them by forcing it to look at the reality of death.

"When I told the priest that I wanted to *know* where he was," commented one widow, "he advised me to say some twenty Hail Marys, attend a full week of Novenas, and to remember the Blessed Virgin's sorrow at seeing her own Son die." Still very distraught after two years, this older woman smoked heavily, though her husband had died of lung cancer and she had spots on her lungs. " 'Father,' I says to him, 'all the Hail Marys in the world won't bring him back. He's all I had. What am I to do?' And he answers, 'My child,'—Jesus, I'm old enough to be his mother —'I am sure that our Blessed Savior took him away to his eternal reward so he would not have to suffer anymore.' With that he hands me a couple of mass cards, tells me he'll pray for the peace of his soul and goes on his way. I see him every Sunday, and he smiles. But he's scared to ask how I am. I can see it." This woman's response is not unusual. Everyone has told her to "get over it," that her dead husband is better off, and none of the clergy she has come into contact with have given her the opportunity to begin to work through her grief.

Each denomination, each variety of religion, seems to

have its own peculiar problems when it comes to dealing with death. One rabbi told me that Judaism deals realistically with death and that there are, as a result, no major problems; but a Jewish woman told me she was cut off from the synagogue because it was through her husband that she had membership in the orthodox body.

Almost without exception widows and widowers, one after the other, have expressed tremendous bitterness toward the clergy. "They forget you, that's what," commented one. Another: "I haven't seen my minister since the day of the funeral except in church." Still another: "I want to begin again, but how? My minister told me to live for my girls." And yet another: "They're worse than doctors. First the doctors won't tell you if he's dead or dying, and then ministers tell you it doesn't matter anyhow." And this bitterness extends into the life of the church—lack of concern of the members, especially in larger parishes, and being left out of almost all social activities of the parish. "We were in the doubles group until Fred died," commented one woman in her late forties, "then I was never asked to another function. I received a sympathy card, but what I needed was to talk to them."

Some clergy do make efforts to talk to the bereaved, but the results are not always helpful. One Methodist minister visited a new widow not to give her moral support for her decision making but to reprimand her because he had heard that she was drinking. Instead of listening to her, he lectured her on the evils of drink. Another minister came to call on a widow about eighteen months after her husband's death, to caution her against jumping into the social scene "too quickly." He then went on with lurid descriptions of how men were waiting at every turn for the vulnerable young widow who needed love. He frightened her so thoroughly that when several months later she became involved with a man, she required and still does require counseling to deal with some of her sexual hang-ups.

"Joe will be watching what you do," the minister had told her, making the dead husband much like some guardian angel.

There are ministers, of course, who are sensitive to bereavement, who really feel that grief is one of the normal processes of life, and who are open toward the variety of ways in which grief is manifested. Unfortunately, when these ministers are in parish work, they often find themselves caught up in commitments which would necessitate a forty-eight-hour day. Some of the ministers, in association with their church school superintendents, try to set up programs that will sensitize people to what is involved in grief. Most of these kinds of programs are planned for adults, however. Children are normally introduced to the societally acceptable theological idea of death rather than to the reality of earthly separation.

I had understood the behavior of Keith's schoolteachers and principal as a total misperception of an event very significant to his own life. I had not expected the same in his Sunday School class, though. I had thought that the death would be openly faced, and Keith and Craig did not miss a Sunday (it seemed to me that to stay away from Sunday School and church even one Sunday would be to negate what I had been pushing, namely, the Christian community as the expression of concern and love). But the Sunday School teachers were unsure about what to say. One young teacher with children of her own told everyone that God had taken Keith's Daddy off to heaven where he was now living with God. Keith told me therefore that his Daddy was not really dead. I told Keith that many people believed in a place called heaven where the souls were with God, yes, but that there were no bodies alive walking around. I further told Keith that if his teacher were talking to an adult she would probably express her beliefs in different terms, that she had oversimplified the whole situation so that children "would understand."

I fumed at the teacher because I had hoped that one thing Keith would get from the whole series of experiences was the understanding that different people dealt with death in different ways. Why had she told them definitively that Bob was not really dead? The dogmatism with which her ideas and attitudes had been presented distressed me. But the Sunday School teacher in question and others in the church school were equally distressed with me. Their responses ranged from "You can't call her a Christian anyway" to "How can you rob the children of hope?"

To me, religion is an attitude rather than a set of beliefs, and it entails being in a constant state of searching. How can we even begin to search for answers unless we begin with the search for questions? I strongly felt that my attitude was biblically sound. Saint Paul points out that "now we see through a glass darkly," which says to me that we cannot ever state with certainty what we may believe with faith. In my calmer moments I could see that it really did not matter what any one person said at any one particular time but that in the long run the responses of the community as a whole would provide the security that we all needed to deal with this event.

It seemed that so many of the problems created and so much of the defensiveness assumed came out of the larger theological framework within which religious teaching for both adults and children is established. Children are surrounded by death on a daily basis. Most of them have seen some form of violent death as part of a television series. And for young children, the line between fantasy and reality is nonexistent. Which death is more realistic to them? And yet, with very few exceptions, the various church curricula tend to ignore death completely. Most ministers I have encountered or have heard of have suggested that young children not attend the funeral or memorial service. I heard about one young child who did, however, but was thoroughly unprepared for it. Seeing her mother's cosmeticized corpse in the casket, she could not understand why it did not move; the open casket perpetuated, in her case, the fantasy handed to her—that her mother had "gone to sleep" at some time. "Now, let's not upset the children" is a common refrain. Children who have not encountered death as a human fact in any sort of structured fashion can well be expected to have problems relating to death when it affects them personally. It seems utterly incredible that we are afraid to discuss death with children because "they might get upset" and at the same time present them with a world full of violence and war and hate.

Much of the problem has to do with seminary training. Several ministers I know have commented that there was no special emphasis on handling grief. One fellow claimed that seminary was a "three-year trip." Another said he got a good deal of experience on how to administer a parish but nothing on how to minister to people. Still another had his first "practical," as he called it, when he was called to fill in for a vacationing pastor his last year of divinity school and realized that he had not even the slightest idea of how to plan a funeral service; he had never seen a book on death, burial, or grief in the entire three years. One prominent divinity school associated with a major medical center has only two courses dealing with "crisis ministry," and they are not offered every year. Within the "theological issues and systematic theology" part of the curriculum, one course is offered on the historic responses to death from the *Epic of Gilgamesh* to Kazantzakis' *Odysseus.* There are courses on sexuality, forgiveness, atonement, various theologians, social ethics, the church as anything and everything—but nothing on death, dying, or grief within theological frameworks. One course outlined dealt with periods of crisis, listing every possible form of crisis except death.

Looking for books dealing with grief and bereavement, I went to a seminary library. Grief was not listed as a subject in the card catalog. Neither was bereavement. I thought about all the religious words I had heard at funerals. Consolation? Sure enough: "Consolation, *see also* Joy and Sorrow." When I looked over the literature my disbelief turned to shock. Most of what the students could read in their seminary library was dated material along the vein of how to offer hope in a time of need, proffering advice on how to tell the bereaved spouse or child that the "departed" (not dead) person was with the heavenly Father and how they ought to "get over" their grief if they have but faith.

The person to whom I felt closest at any one time during that first week was no clergyman but another widow. Had anyone told me before Bob died of the bond that death could create between us, I would have probably arched my eyebrow and said, "Come on, now. We have nothing in common." But that sense of knowing she *knew* how I felt, that she understood the sense of utter despair through all the nit-and-pick work that first week, was everything to me then.

One minister I know always refers any newly widowed person to someone else who has worked through his grief. He considers that way of "helping" to be integral to his ministry. I was touched when he asked me to call a newly widowed member of his parish. Most ministers who have done this are usually at their wit's end, or openly admit they want nothing to do with the problem. One man asked me to call a member of his parish because he "just didn't know what to say." When I asked him why he had to *say* anything, he responded, "But I'm supposed to console him." Another minister, more cynical, admitted feeling that he was spouting empty pieties, "but that's what they want, and that's what I give." "Tell me where he is," a woman had said to him. "Just tell me you know he's with

God, and I'll be content." "I told her that he was with God, but I think she thought I was lying through my teeth. And I was," he admitted.

Many of the widowed people I have come into contact with over the past year and a half said that they felt the clergy had never listened to them, only talked at them. Some of the responsibility here lies with the laity, who may act as if the clergy were there to console them, to feed them the words of assurance. Many of us want to avoid the catharsis after catharsis that must be experienced, and so we turn to the clergy in the blind hope that maybe, just maybe, they will have some magic formula that will quickly alleviate the pain. And when they cannot provide such, we turn against them in bitterness.

The clergy who do not follow up after the first week normally are too caught up in the pressures of administering their parishes. When the newly widowed person is asked at the front door of the church, "How are you doing," and the answer comes back, "Good" or "Okay" or "I'll make it," the clergyperson can think, that's one more problem I won't have to deal with. He is so pressed that he simply cannot engage in intensive dialogue on the front steps before the entire congregation, and normally he will not "come to call," a practice that seems to be peculiarly Protestant.

The Roman Catholic clergy seem to be even more caught up in administering parishes, possibly because of the larger physical plants a typical Catholic parish entails. Those normally credited as being the most sensitive are the teaching sisters in Catholic schools who meet the children of the family in an everyday situation. One man who felt that the priests were "useless" had nothing but warmth for the sisters of the school which his daughters attended. They asked after the family, planned special treats for the children in the family, took on a special mothering role because they knew how deeply the family was suffering from the loss. This same man, clearly in a state of intense grief, never heard from his priest, who commented to another member of the parish that he "must be doing okay because he still comes to 8:00 A.M. mass every Sunday, just as before."

One Protestant woman commented ruefully, "I had to stay away from church for over a month before my minister would call on me." The clergy and the laity of churches expect the intensely grieving to exhibit different forms of social behavior: if the newly widowed do not come to church or drop out of social groups, then it is because they "just can't face people," and the congregation responds by isolating them even further.

Many of the clergy openly admit that they feel to send a "lay" person constitutes a threat to their self-image. "I was trained to deal with all these things," remarked one minister. "I don't need some meddling little old lady to 'help' me out." This same pastor prided himself on how well he administered his big city parish, but he was utterly neglectful of the mourning members in it. One minister, who feels good if he can just "help out," has built up a system of referrals, and in his mostly older congregation uses the widowed to talk to the widowed. In some communities this use of the widowed to help the widowed has become organized. Part of the reluctance of some clergy to do this comes from their feeling that a newly widowed person may not want to talk to a "perfect stranger." But "outreach" organizations for the newly widowed in various parts of the country, which have been working without any clergy referrals, have indicated over a 75 percent acceptance of "help."

Chaplains in hospitals deal with death directly but often just initially. There are some hospitals which have established "counseling centers" to which people may come in times of crisis. Several widowed persons I know use such counseling centers because they feel they cannot discuss their grief with their local clergy. Sometimes, if a death through a long illness has established a relationship of trust between chaplain and family, it enables the bereaved to trust the chaplain with their grief. Unfortunately, there seems to be little connection between the various chaplains and the parish clergy in the same general community. One does not relate to the other. In a Roman Catholic hospital of a middle-sized community, not one of the chaplains had ever met the local parish priests.

Much of the lack of communication stems from inter- and intradenominational differences. It takes a great deal of energy to work through interdenominational problems, to reach out beyond the parish. The attempts made have been in response to blatant social problems. In many of the "para-social" areas, such as drug control and the like, separate structures have been established which operate independently of the churches and the ministry, though an individual church or minister may be involved. But generally grieving is not seen in relation to such problems. Rarely do we hear someone say, "She was fine until her husband died." Normally, the reaction is, "She was fine until she started drinking." She was not "fine." She was probably grieving intensely and simply could not find the support needed during the period of working through the grief.

But if the clergy and the religious communities are incapable of facing death, they are doubly fearful of the combination of death and sexuality. This area cannot begin to be approached by the clergy who do not even approach death and grief openly. Even in the widowed-to-widowed caregiving a certain level of trust is required before one can turn to the other and ask, "Do you feel this way?"

If the religious community—both professional and lay—is to deal with death and grieving, they must be prepared to deal with all the complex and heavy issues of life and living. The clergy, through seminary education and continuing education, should be opened up to the phenomena of grief, the varieties of responses, and the validity of those responses. Much of our puritanical sexual morality must be examined and loosened up so that honest feelings can be acknowledged. The standard theological responses to death, the connection of grief and sexual needs, and the sheer loneliness that accompanies grief must be explored further. Telling someone that the "departed" have gone off to a better place does not erase the grief, the pain, and the sense of aloneness that the widowed feel. Grief must be accepted as more than a dark night of the soul. The clergy must learn to listen, and to talk less. And they, as well as we laypeople, must face the question of individual deaths and build a theology that makes those deaths acceptable to us all so that life can be lived more abundantly.

9

Accommodations

Everyday trivial issues, minute concerns, seem to pile up one by one, then in clumps, until one is standing knee-deep in them. They begin the very first week with the very first "How will you . . . ?" At times I thought that handling the big issues was easier than managing the day-to-day decisions, hassling with the sitters, setting this or that up, making arrangements, making accommodations. But a major decision sends off shock waves in the form of the thousands of minute considerations which make up the details of living.

One of my early decisions was to take in a college student who would be able to watch the boys—a live-in sitter, since my classes ran during the dinner hour and I already knew the difficulty of getting a sitter for even a single class once a week. First, I had to make preparations for the student. Those preparations entailed cleaning out the library, which had also served as my workroom, sewing room, television room, and general storage area. I had thought about donating the bulk of Bob's history collection to the library "someday." That "someday" was to come sooner than I had expected. I was faced with the task of cleaning out a collection of several thousand volumes, half of which would come out of Bob's study and the other half of which would have to come out of the library to make room for the student's bed. Bit by bit I separated the books which were to go from those I would keep in what was now becoming my study.

Before I donated any books, however, I decided that Bob's friends ought to have first choice, so friend by friend, books were picked out. Then I had to go through the hassle of getting the college library to take the rest. As I was soon to discover, one simply does not donate a collection to a library. I boxed up the books, wrote the required form letters, and waited for the library to come and get the books. But by the middle of August a process which had begun in early June had clearly bogged down. I was becoming impatient. Books were piled up on the floor, I was tripping over them, and I wanted some area cleared before school started. I talked to the librarian, then to her administrative superior. Due to administrative squabbling over library responsibilities, the books remained in the study. Finally, I lost patience, called the college president, and told him that the books had better be picked up or I would donate them elsewhere. At last they were removed.

Another consequence of the simple decision to take in a student was the cleaning of closets which held the physical effects and memories of ten years. This meant everything had to be thoroughly examined; and it also required the organization of what was to be kept into albums and boxes which then had to be labeled. Though it was emotionally purging, it was also sometimes emotionally shattering. Besides the cathartic experience of cleaning out, the amount of time invested was stupendous. Bob's notes, dating back to his own undergraduate courses, had to be perused. At times I felt as if I had never seen so much paper—or thrown away so much paper. Bob was the pack rat personified. He had kept his class notes from other instructors, other students' notes from the same instructors, and notes on the comparisons. Most of his own lectures I shared with his friends, who felt deeply touched at receiving them.

The storage bureau in the student's room had to be cleaned out. It contained winter storage in summer and vice versa. Bob's clothing had already gone to a local "halfway house" via a funneling service agency in New Haven. But where to put my things, and the children's things, and the extra materials I had not yet used in sewing? And the sewing machine? I then went about looking for a secondhand sewing cabinet, new cabinets being outrageously expensive. Then I had to rearrange the furniture in my bedroom to make room for the cabinet. All of the out-of-season clothing was moved; the extra material was then stored. Finally, the television had to go. First, the antenna cables would not quite make it across the house to come through the window of the other room. Second, moving the television set necessitated a new antenna because of reception problems. And, third, that other room was my study. Another accommodation, then, was a partial surrender of "my" study to the children for their television shows.

I knew there would have to be some changes in the household routine to enable the incoming student to adjust more easily. The children would not have the free range of the household. Accommodations would have to be made, adjustments in my own lifestyle. I could not wander as freely, talk as freely. After she moved in, I felt as if I were always wearing a mask. One of my friends remarked, "Oh, it must be nice to have someone to talk to." In one way, I could talk to the student, but in another, deeper, way, I could not. She was ten years my junior. She had totally different values. I felt as if I were never quite alone. I made some mistakes in initially establishing our relationship, of course, one of which was trying to treat her as my equal. As a result, at times she seemed to take advantage of what she considered to be my largesse and of what I considered was plain human decency and the assumption that a twenty-year-old was responsible for her own decisions and their consequences.

For the first few weeks after Bob's death I continued to go to bed on the schedule I had kept before his death. The first night that I awoke at three I thought, this will soon stop. However, it did not stop as soon as I thought it would, and as a consequence my whole pattern of activities shifted. I became an aficionado of late-night movies. My friends simply could not believe that where I had always fallen asleep at nine-thirty or ten, I now never went to bed before one or two. But I needed to do things. So I cleaned. I cleaned out files, and I cleaned out papers. I threw out papers, saved papers, sorted them, arranged them. After the cleaning was done I filed and filed. I worked on sorting out Bob's dissertation notes. His colleagues were asking me to "do something" with them. They seemed to be uncertain of my role; I felt as if they wanted me to stay somewhere between oblivion and the vision of the weeping, wailing widow. (Just don't weep near me, please.) I would work in the yard during the day just to get by until the evening, when I could be alone and feel that I was doing something. At times I felt as if the work were aimless. At other times it seemed somewhat productive.

The biggest accommodations in my lifestyle arose from the whole business of child-care. During the fall, child-care was arranged for during my classes and I felt good about that. I was able to stay up at school and study after class twice a week. Child-care assumed a special importance in my life. It meant that any time I wanted to do *anything* myself I had to arrange for a sitter. Study, thesis research, shopping, and meetings all required child-care. I could no longer just go to a movie. I did not go out socially except when obliged to do so. I found that I could not go swimming by myself, could not ice skate, could not do this or that. I went through a protracted argument with the people at Keith's school over whether or not he could stay for lunch. Lunch space was provided for the children of working mothers, but not student mothers.

But the weekends were the hardest and the deadest. The Saturdays were especially difficult for the children because other families were doing things as families and the children were not really sure whether the three of us constituted a family. Also, Saturday evenings were especially lonely for me because I knew that my friends were off together somewhere, perhaps telling themselves how unfortunate my situation was and wasn't it sad, etc. The history department invited me to their annual summer party but I felt very uncomfortable because no one wanted to talk to me except about the death. I was tired of talking about Bob's death. I wanted to discuss politics, ideas, issues, almost anything else. Several of them would stand around me, staring silently. I felt as if there were social expectations which I (the widow) was not fulfilling.

I found that my living patterns depended on others more than I had previously thought possible. And I also found that my living depended on money but not in the same way as before. Our living standard had changed. We no longer "entertained," nor were we entertained. We had mixed in a circle of faculty and their wives, gone out with them, discussed issues and people, and enjoyed each other's company. All that was done. I craved adult company and at the same time wanted to be alone. Though friends were open and wanted me to feel welcome, "we" no longer were. So my circle of friends grew more intense, and narrowed to those who accepted me apart from "us."

I also felt utterly responsible. Somehow I felt as if life and death in the house depended on me. I was afraid of having a social drink because I felt so responsible. People, sensing this, were constantly offering advice. The advice ranged from "Go home" (I was home, damn it! I would respond) to "Stay here" and from "Get a live-in student—as terrible as they are" to "Oh, don't get a student—they're all hippies." People would intrude into my world with their advice on life, love, money, sex, children, religion, parents, moving furniture, painting rooms, almost every conceivable topic. Even if I met someone for the first time, that person, upon learning of my "widowed status," would with equanimity offer advice on any possible topic.

There seem to be two major sorts of accommodations—those of external behavior observed by society, and those of the heart. The external and societal patterns extended to the smallest details; but the accommodations of the heart were emotionally consuming. Apart from the aloneness, the empty house, the lack of adults with whom to talk, and the general feeling that by five in the afternoon, I could climb the walls—apart from the grief, the greatest internal accommodation was living without love. Gone from my life was the sense of commitment to another human being at the level of emotional intimacy necessary in marriage. Others I have spoken to have referred to this lack as "the hole" in their lives. It is the sense of not having an anchor, of floating endlessly, without a pivot by which to gauge oneself.

I realized how few were the external accommodations I had made. Some newly widowed persons find themselves forced to move, totally alter their children's surroundings, and sometimes drastically reduce their living standard. For men, there is the adjustment to be made in learning how to take care of a household, how to do the laundry, the cooking, and take care of the children. There are major shifts in living patterns and locations for many.

For me, as the year progressed, the accommodations, though not reduced in number, lessened in immediacy. For some the sense of urgency and desperation is not mitigated. For some life is just as intensely painful one year later as it was the first week. Much of that may come from not having accepted the innumerable cathartic experiences offered by everyday existence and using them as positive experiences for growing and continuing to live.

10

After One Year

I had not seen Bruce in almost eight years. He had been the assistant minister of the church in which Bob and I were married. "Let me look at you," he said. "How about a hug?" I threw my arms around him and sobbed out, "It's been one hell of a year!" "Yeah, I bet." And then I started to talk. After one year, what do you say? What do you say in a few hours to a person you haven't seen in eight years? You begin at the beginning and recount as much as you can.

As I talked about the past sixteen months I could say it had been a period of real growing and of self-discovery. But I must have also used a lot of time just in describing the despair and depressions I had experienced. Those sixteen months had not been divided neatly between the sense of growing and the despair, but included both, often simultaneously. I often felt exhilarated by my own process of change, and utterly despairing and lonely at the same time. There were occasions when I would say something to someone and think, did I really say that? Does that ever sound gushy! At other times I would cut so hard into someone that I felt as if I were murdering the soul. And, there would be occasions on which after an intense care-giving session on either an individual or group basis I would sit back and hear a "professional"—cleric, doctor, or psychiatrist—tell me how well I had "gotten over" my grief.

I have certainly learned a lot about myself. At times it seems as if I have learned more than I care to know. I have learned that I am afraid of certain kinds of life commitments while sometimes I have been all-too-anxious to jump into them. After a series of dates, which developed into a rather intense relationship within a short period of time, I realized that the whole appeal of that developing relationship was that the person in question could only visit New Haven several times a year. That meant a freedom to be intense when he was here, but that the distance precluded a sustained growth and development of that relationship which might prove threatening.

There were nights when I sat down to "work" surrounded with enough food to feed an army. That was deliberate, I now realize. I had become consumed with my own sense of grief and with each sensation accompanying it, as if each sensation was a way of grasping on to life itself. Eating became my link to life. One weekend, after my parents had visited me and commented that I was getting fat—and therefore less desirable to men—I went on a total eating binge. As I began to feel less oppressed by what my parents said to me, about what they thought about my weight, appearance, and demeanor, I stopped eating. Eating was also a way of making myself unattractive to men. As I gained confidence in my ability to handle social or sexual situations, as I began to like myself again, I stopped the eating. The progressions were small and sporadic.

People would say to me, "You need to start over, to begin again." In one sense there was no "starting over," though each morning I would wake up and say to myself, "This is a new day." It took a long time until I began to believe that statement. Despair, the feeling that "this day is like every other," and loneliness enveloped my being. I would seek out new and challenging—though not too challenging—situations in the hope that some new experience would inject life into what had become for me a very sterile world. I gained an expectation of the unexpected.

Only one month after Bob died I visited some old friends in Massachusetts, and went with them to their Unitarian church in Arlington. The minister talked about the sense of the common life, as experienced through friendship, the necessity of opening oneself up to what friends could offer. Combined with a meditation from Nietzsche on death, a reading from Tillich's *Courage to Be,* and a sermon on being open to critical times in our individual and corporate lives in order to be more sensitive to the messages given by those times, the impact of the service was overwhelming. My friends could literally feel me tremble.

Sermons often seemed to coincide with my own understanding of myself and to focus on those issues I was wrestling with at a given time. Listening to a sermon on the necessity of accepting one's own limitations contributed to my own acceptance of myself as a human being before God and other human beings. I had been driving myself in my church commitments to somehow justify my existence, and I found that accepting my own existence and my "living space," as I called it, produced a deeper and less frenetic commitment to the church community and an inner sense of purpose. That sermon occurred at a time when I was struggling with plans for the future. The unexpected result at that time was the extension of my understanding of myself from the context of the church community to the context of my professional life as a librarian.

As I began looking for a job, there were opportunities both in Connecticut and elsewhere. Through midwinter I seemed to be grasping for straws at jobs elsewhere in the country. But the unexpected kept happening. Friends and strangers would say things to me about some subject which seemed unrelated but which offered me a new perspective on what I was doing. For a while almost every conversation took on a special significance in terms of my sense of what I was about, what I was thinking, or what my children were thinking and how they were responding to the proposed move. In the end I decided to stay in New Haven, not because it was easier but because the commitments that I had made to the community reflected my deepest commitments and because as I observed the reactions of my children to the talk of moving I saw what would be best for them.

I began to listen very carefully to the ways in which people discussed "coping with death." The choice of words like "coping," "getting over," "adjusting," or "recovering" reflected the attitudes of those who have not experienced death from the perspective of a widow or widower. What was most intriguing to me was the way in which the widowed person reflected societal attitudes toward grief and grieving to the point of incorporating the vocabulary. One night a group of widowed friends were sitting in my living room for a discussion. Finally, someone said, "I don't like that word 'cope.' And 'recover' makes me sound like I'm sick." As we discussed our feelings more deeply, someone else ventured the idea that one does not "recover" from grief but takes the whole experience and uses it as a basis for a deeper understanding of oneself. Whether the marriage was good or bad, whether the death was sudden or expected, and whether the grieving was carried to the deepest of intensities or not, all these experiences could nevertheless give us better understandings of ourselves as human beings.

To be sure, the fact that we are able to see our lives as continuing—not "starting over" as if the past is to be erased—does not eradicate the loneliness. But it does give us the courage to admit we are lonely, that we need to be needed, and that we need to care about someone and to have someone care about us. The need to care and to be cared for can involve a friend, a new marital situation, our children, or any one of a number of things. The need to be needed is extremely important because it means that *we* are essential to someone else's existence and that other person's understanding of himself. We need to know that we can give something to someone else as well as get it. Admitting our loneliness comes hard to many of us. I know that to admit that I am desperately lonely is, for me, to say that I am vulnerable and open to being hurt. But each new risk in the direction of commitment seems worth any possible hurt. If through the hurt and disappointment of any commitment—whether it is with men or women—I am not only honestly able to say but to act on the belief that I can use these experiences to deepen my understanding of myself, then the commitment has been worth the risk and the risk worth whatever consequences.

There were times over the year that I felt autonomous and apart from others. There were times during which I felt superior to other people, convinced I could "go it alone." But over the course of the year the fabric of individual and social involvement was woven around me to the point that I realized that to pull one of the strands would be to tear the fabric. Over the course of the year the "bad" experiences were put into perspective. Additionally I learned that to admit that I needed other people was not to make me less human but more so.

Over the past year and a half I have tried various ways of facing the loss and loneliness. Accepting the "reality" of Bob's death was the easiest thing to do. When one sees a dead body it becomes obvious that one cannot do anything to change that particular situation. I searched out new relationships with people knowing that no relationship with any one other person would be the same as that with Bob.

But no relationship with any person is what it is with any other person. Over the fits and starts of a year or so, the intensity of the loss descends upon one at some of the most unexpected times. But at each point, the experience is different from the initial impact, from that first night in that all-too-big bed, alone.

I expected the first "anniversary" to be hard. I wondered who would remember the day. I was afraid of spending that time alone, so I dropped some hints and one friend picked them up and invited us to dinner that night. After dinner and putting the boys to bed, we went to a hearing on a new high school because I felt the need to commit myself to the future instead of living in the past. I had received no indication from members of my family that they remembered. One person who did remember was another widow. The next day I saw her car out front and excitedly greeted her. I could only sputter, "You remembered!" She nodded that she knew what that date meant to me. We talked about the year, and as she left, she turned to me and said, "Happy new year." That's right! I thought. It *is* a new year. It was incredible what that statement came to mean to me as I ruminated with friends about the year and a whole new perspective opened up.

Another person who remembered the anniversary was Bob's sister. I had put off calling her and finally did later that week, to hear her say that she had not phoned because she had not wanted to "intrude." Intrude? Oh no, no intrusion. I felt as if some load had been removed from me. We talked for a good half hour and shared our grief and feelings together as we had never done. That closeness was good for both of us, we felt.

The week after the first-year date I commented to friends, "Well, it's been a year." I was surprised by the responses: "Has it been a year *already?*" "Time certainly does fly," said one colleague's wife. Already? Time flying? I felt as if it had been an eternity measurable in seconds. My sense of time, when it came to this, was a jumble.

The unexpected pangs of loneliness are what hit me the hardest. Walking on the beach at Plymouth, where we had honeymooned, brought up myriad confused feelings. Earlier that day I had gone by the gravesite at Brockton and felt nothing. I guess I do not associate Bob with a physical place but with experiences and feelings and relationships. For example, I remember that it wasn't the "first date" after Bob's death that was the hardest, but the third, because my date took me to one of those fifties musicals which related so much to Bob's world. Funerals are not difficult for me to attend, but a celebration of the spirit of unity in a downtown church was very hard for me. Watching political programs on television, watching the Watergate hearings, and being involved in the world are hard. I wanted so much to laugh with Bob at some of Senator Ervin's comments, cry over political defeats with him, and share the world in which we had been involved.

Everyone seems to have his own ritual to get him through those experiences which affect him most deeply. I have developed my little rituals, the manifestation of my confrontation with ultimate power and reality. Those rituals reveal much of what and who I am. There are times when I feel the bottom of my life is falling out, that in either my thinking or behavior I have hit the ultimate in deprivation, and then I listen to others and realize that they have the same feelings, too. One of my rituals is listening to the problems and difficulties of others. Another has been just to hold on to people who are lonely because I know that I need to be held on to when I am lonely. Verbal rituals are also important. I have now said "happy new year" to others and seen that it has affected them as it did me. Just as we confess we also receive absolution in our own eyes. The equivalent of that absolution has been that statement seriographed so beautifully by Corita Kent: "To believe in God is to know that all the rules will be fair and that there will be wonderful surprises." Amen.